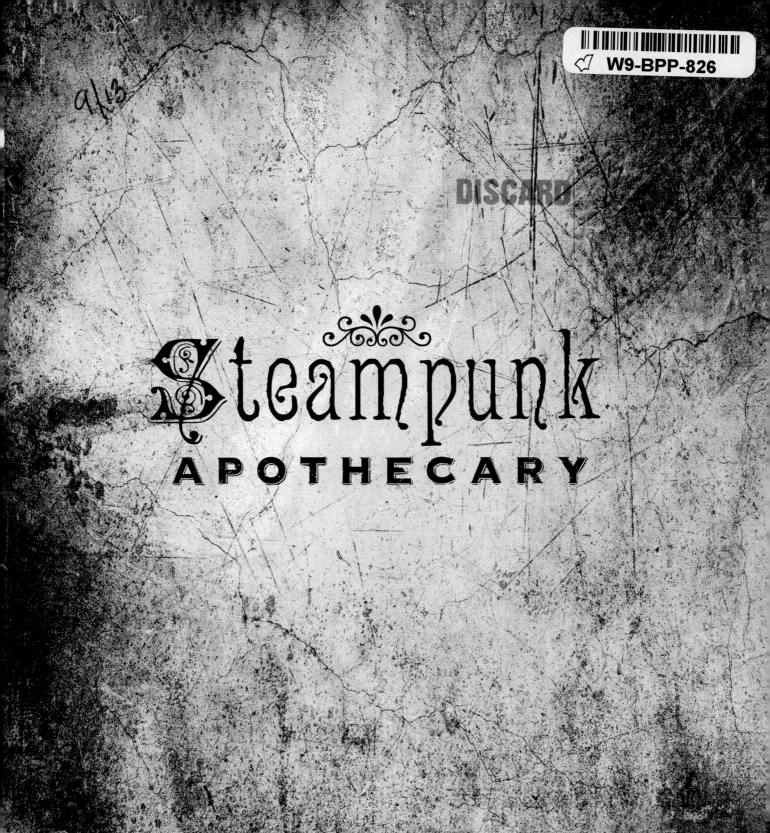

Steampunk
APOTHECARY

Steampunk

APOTHECARY

CREATE ENCHANTING JEWELLERY AND ACCESSORIES

Jema 'Emilly Ladybird' Hewitt

THE GUILD OF MASTER CRAFTSMAN PUBLICATIONS

First published 2013 by
Guild of Master Craftsman Publications Ltd
Castle Place, 166 High Street, Lewes,
East Sussex BN7 1XU

ISBN 978 1 86108 975 5

Publisher: Jonathan Bailey
Production Manager: Jim Bulley
Managing Editor: Gerrie Purcell
Senior Project Editor: Wendy McAngus
Editor: Judith Chamberlain-Webber
Managing Art Editor: Gilda Pacitti
Designer: Rob Janes

Chapter opener and step-by-step photography:
Jema Hewitt (digital artist: Terry Lightfoot)
Project photography: Martin SoulStealer
(art director: Jema Hewitt)

Colour origination by GMC Reprographics
Printed and bound in China

Dedication

For Nik, who doesn't believe in faeries, and in
loving memory of Harry, Worthington and Emily,
who always believed in chocolate buttons.

You are cordially invited
to join adventuress

Miss Emilly Ladybird

and her faithful family retainer,

Mr Woppit,

as they head off on a fantastical journey of discovery.

While searching out strange artefacts
for her employers

Dickens and Rivett,

Emilly will encounter an array of astounding
characters and visions…

CONTENTS

EMBARK ON YOUR STEAMPUNK ADVENTURE

✳ VAMPIRE CHATEAU

✳ LABYRINTH LIBRARY

INTRODUCTION

Fairy tales allow us to step into a world of magic and mayhem, where the impossible can become reality, teaching us something about life and people along the way. Steampunk, rather than relying on magic to provide a fantastical solution, turns to science. Victorian science, to be precise. It provides a wonderful daydream of imaginary Victorian steam technology that enabled an alternate timeline of Victorians to have adventures that are every bit as improbable and outlandish as those of a fairy tale...

Steampunk as a genre has come a very long way since I wrote my first magazine article on it in 2007. It has become an established style for mainstream crafting, and an explosion of events and conventions has ensured constant media coverage of the people who participate in the fun. Its influences have been seen on high-street fashions and TV shows, sometimes subtly, sometimes not. But debates still rage about what steampunk actually is. Is it a literary movement? An artistic style? A musical subculture? Should it be light-hearted fun or taken very seriously?

I believe it is all of these, and much more. Steampunk, by blending the past with the future, has created a new world and a new community where imagination and exploration rule. There are amazing conventions across the world, where steampunks gather in gorgeous Victorian-inspired costume, to talk, shop, drink tea, debate, learn and listen to music; 'steampunk' is used as a tagline on practically every craft product that uses a distressed or vintage look, and many bookstores have a specific steampunk fiction section. It seems no matter what your age or interest, steampunk is inspiring everyone.

Perhaps it is the combination of that which we know and are familiar with – Victorian fashion, history, cake and good manners – with the wow factor of the unknown, the science fiction 'what-if' element. This allows steampunk to delve into the realms of fantasy, to transform from Victorian re-enactment into something new. We can rewrite history, keeping the elements we love and ditching the parts we no longer feel affinity with. This means everybody's experience of steampunk is different; just like the punk movement of the 1970s, it's about individuality, taking the parts you love and making something new and unique with them.

This book is a blend of dark fairy tales and steampunk adventures, a fantasy in a parallel world where magic and technology walk hand in hand. I hope you enjoy following me down the rabbit hole.

Emilly Ladybird

C. Risch-Lau
BREGENZ.

FAIRY HUNTER

Roaming through Cottingly Wood with Miss Peacey,
I was quickly overwhelmed with the scent of the trees
— a damp green smell that tried to lull me into a happy doze.
Fortunately, Miss P is an old hand at these types of expeditions
and had a couple of handkerchiefs bathed in eau de cologne
at the ready. Sneezing, I opened my phantasmagorical device
and started to look for weak spots between the worlds.

Concentrating hard, I looked for the shimmering dust in the shafts of sunlight
and watched the needle of the device whirl in giddying circles. Then, just as
I thought I'd found a good thin spot, I noticed Mr Woppit disappearing into the
dark gap of a hollow tree. Obviously, I chased after him as he was carrying
the luncheon basket and no one wants to hunt fairies while hungry, do they?

As I hurled myself through the gap in the trunk I was able to grab
both him and the basket. I then continued my explorations after a stern
warning to Mr Woppit not to go running off. However, everything seemed
curiously different; some of the trees had odd-coloured leaves, there
were flowers and butterflies I didn't recognise, and now I can
hear music drifting through the trees...

FAIRYSTONE PENDANT

When attempting to catch fairies, it does help if you can remain
unaffected by their glamour… Although the exact technical
specification of this stone is unknown, Miss Peacey, Naturalist,
Artist and Collector, has used it to enormous effect to
increase her assortment of curios.

Other important pieces of equipment include a large soft net and a
collecting jar. Miss Peacey is one of the few mortals to have returned
unscathed from the fae realm. She even declined the advances of Oberon
himself, stating that, 'his moustache was insufficiently well formed'.

Her eventual escape from the shadow lands was effected
by a string of bunting, half a quart of gin and some
peppermints in a pretty tin.

FAIRYSTONE PENDANT

❖ SUPPLIES

- Small amounts of polymer clay (brown, black, white, translucent, pearl and blue)

- Liquid polymer clay

- Piece of trailing vine filigree

- Large cog

- Several small watch parts

- Tiny screws or cut-down headpins

- Acrylic paints or patina solution

- Renaissance wax or compatible varnish

- 2 metal bead caps

- Eyepin

- 5mm jumpring

❖ EQUIPMENT

- Pasta machine or small acrylic rolling pin
- Scalpel and tissue blade
- ¾in (2cm) round cutter
- Flat-nose pliers
- Tweezers
- Small, deep baking tray
- Cornflour
- Medium wet and dry sandpaper
- Superfine-grade sandpaper
- Dust mask
- Buffing wheel (optional)
- Round-nose pliers
- Paintbrush
- Pin

1 Condition the colours for the mixtures by rolling and kneading the clay between your fingers until soft and pliable. Mix the colours as follows until almost blended, but leave a bit of marbling for a stone-like look.

Mix 1: A walnut-sized piece each of brown, black, white and a pea-sized piece of translucent.

Mix 2: Half of mix 1 plus a hazelnut-sized piece of pearl and a pea-sized piece of translucent.

Mix 3: A hazelnut-sized piece each of blue and translucent.

Roll out mixes 1 and 2, with a pasta machine or an acrylic rolling pin, to ½in (1mm) thick and layer into a stripy slab about 2½in (7cm) long, 2in (5cm) wide and ½in (1cm) deep.

2 Use a tissue blade to shape the stone into an irregular triangle. Tissue blades are very sharp so be sure it's the right way up. Bend the blade then cut down into the clay with one stroke. Remove the centre hole with the round cutter. Go around the shape with a scalpel, trimming the edges so they are rounded – don't forget the back. Gently roll the cut-out circle into a bead and make a hole through it with a pin.

3 To make a realistic band of blue quartz, roll out mix 3 to ⅛in (3mm) thick. Cut your grey slab in two places and dab a fine smear of liquid clay across each cut. Gently squeeze the grey slab back together with strips of blue clay sandwiched in between. Bond grey to blue, wiping away any liquid clay that seeps out. Trim any surplus blue clay neatly with a scalpel. Leave to rest somewhere cool for an hour at least.

Mr Rivett suggests...

A small hand drill is a wonderful tool for speeding up the initial sanding process if your shape is a bit rough or lumpy. Use a small, medium-grade sandpaper attachment and make sure to keep the tool moving, pressing very lightly. You can always take more off, but you cannot replace over-sanded areas.

Pages from the Notebook...

To gain the perfect glossy finish of a polished stone, you'll need to use a small bench grinder with a buffing wheel made from unstitched cotton cloth. Tie back all loose clothing and hair and hold the clay firmly just under the bottom quarter of the wheel, ready for the soft edge of the cloth to polish it. Start the grinding machine and gently bring your piece up to touch the cloth. You just want it to caress the edge with no pressure at all. Polish to a smooth shine and move onto another part. If you press too hard, it will go matt again.

4 Once you have a great-shaped stone, insert your mechanical pieces into the clay. Use the flat-nose pliers to curve the filigree into a shape that will fit around one of the long sides. Place it loosely around the clay, then gently squeeze with the pliers to close around and grip the clay. Cut slits and place the cog and other pieces halfway in, smoothing the clay around them afterwards. Using the tweezers, press smaller bits directly into the clay, adding small screws or headpins to hold them down.

5 Place the piece halfway deep in cornflour to support it as it bakes. Cook, along with the bead, according to your brand of clay's instructions. Allow to cool. Sand with the lowest-grade sandpaper first, gradually working your way up through the grades to a very fine sanding paper. Always wear a dust mask and sand your piece in a bowl filled with water, dipping it in every so often to wash off the dust and make a better surface. Either leave with a satin finish or use a buffing wheel to shine (see notebook left).

6 Use patina or paint combinations to add interest to the metal areas (see page 168). For paint, put plenty on, then wipe it off the raised areas, leaving colour in the recesses. For patinas, wait until dry, then gently sand off with superfine-grade papers to reveal the metal. Seal with Renaissance wax or compatible varnish. To finish, thread your bead on an eyepin with the bead caps each side. Make a top loop, trim and attach to the cog with the jumpring.

USEFUL ADVICE

Polymer clay can mimic almost any other material, including all sorts of rocks and stones. To get a realistic-looking faux rock, look at a few stones to see how their colours mix and change. Mix up different bits of clay and try different ways of layering and combining them to copy your real stones.

Adding different amounts of translucent clay to the mixes will give the rocks a glassy sheen, but you can also add flecks of colour with inclusions of finely grated baked clay, coffee powder or finely chopped unbaked clay. Try adding pearlescent clay or mica powder to give a glittering sheen. Used carefully, even bits of glitter can add realism.

CLOCKWORK BEETLE
CRAVAT PIN

When Professor Van Vaas postulated his thesis on the use of rainbow prisms to open gateways between worlds, he little considered that iridescent wings might serve the same purpose, both for fairies and the little creatures that serve them.

Clockwork beetles are the messengers between the worlds; scurrying hither and thither, they carry messages from the fairy realm to this and back again, so beware if you are tempted to capture one and keep it in a matchbox for your own amusement. Who knows what peace treaties, love letters and party invitations might go astray?

CLOCKWORK BEETLE CRAVAT PIN

❖ SUPPLIES

- Approximately 6in (15cm) 0.8mm (SWG 22, AWG 21) antique bronze or brass-coloured wire

- Assorted cogs and watch parts, plus a few tiny crystals

- Cravat stick pin and guard

- 2-part epoxy putty, such as Geomfix Designer Clay

- A pair of jewel beetle wings (see Mr Dickens's suggestion for alternatives, overleaf)

- Approximately 2in (5cm) Jones Tones Foil Paper

- Iridescent blue/green powder, such as Perfect Pearls Pigment Powder

- Adhesive putty or modelling clay

❖ EQUIPMENT

- A pair of vinyl/latex gloves
- Cutting pliers
- Cocktail stick/modelling tool

  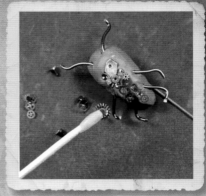

1 Put on the pair of latex or vinyl gloves to protect your hands. Take equal, pea-sized amounts of epoxy putty and blend thoroughly. It will stay soft for about an hour so there's no hurry. Roll it into a teardrop shape, press onto the pad part of your cravat pin and smooth a little putty over the pad for strength. Flatten the top surface slightly and allow to dry.

2 To make the legs, cut the wire into six 1in (2.5cm) lengths and bend them into shape. Mix up pea-sized pieces of epoxy putty as before, then spread a thin layer across the flat top surface, using a cocktail stick or modelling tool to neaten as necessary. Push the legs into position so they sit at the sides of the soft new putty.

3 Start placing your cogs and pieces onto the putty, pressing down to fix firmly. Keep important pieces central and on the lower part of the body as the edges and top part will be covered by the wings. Be careful not to move the delicate little legs out of position at this point. Add the crystals into any gaps to add sparkle and texture. For a very manly pin, use dark colours that will simply twinkle in the light, and for a more flamboyant piece use a brighter but still toning selection.

4 Allow the piece to dry, sticking it into a piece of adhesive putty or modelling clay to keep it still and safe. Take another pea-sized mix of epoxy putty to make the head section. To add colour, press a tiny square of Jones Tones Foil Paper to the epoxy putty, and remove the plastic carry layer after a minute or so. Press the head onto the top of the body and use modelling tools or a cocktail stick to work the two sections together so it looks like one piece and is nice and secure.

Pages from the Notebook...

Building up the pieces in stages, allowing each section to dry thoroughly in between, ensures that you always have a nice firm base to work on. It may take longer, but you'll find it is much easier to get a really professional finish this way than trying to sculpt floppy clay, insert cogs and control a pin that keeps coming loose all at the same time.

Use tweezers or needle-pointed pliers to pick up small cogs and watch parts. Tiny gems are best captured using a tiny bead of adhesive putty on a cocktail stick.

Mr Dickens suggests...

If you do not care to use real beetle wings, or indeed are having trouble finding some, then a large false nail, cut in half, each side shaped with a file and painted with iridescent polish, will make an excellent substitute. Use a large piece of putty to support the wing on your work surface while you paint.

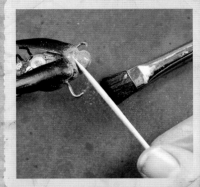

6 Dust the head with iridescent powder to add colour and shine over the foil layer. Remember you can keep adjusting for a good 15 minutes so make sure all the positioning and sculpting is perfect before leaving the final beetle to dry.

5 While the epoxy putty is still soft, slide the wing cases into position, pressing the top edges into the head part and resculpting as necessary. Pop tiny pieces of epoxy putty under the wings to hold them in shape at the top.

THE KEY TO ELFLAND NECKLACE

In the darkest part of the forest, Emilly noticed a little doorway cut into a huge oak tree. An elegant sign hung upon the door proclaimed it 'Open!' Slowly, she pushed the door wide, revealing a glorious display of trinkets, knick-knacks and shiny things.

The sun began to set and shadows danced in the corners as she looked around, then Emilly spotted a pretty necklace, dancing with dewdrops and a tiny key. 'How perfect and pretty! It will be just the thing for Fuchsia Begonia's birthday.'

Emilly looked around for the owner to pay, but only a little tabby cat seemed to be in charge…

THE KEY TO ELFLAND NECKLACE

❖ SUPPLIES

- Approximately 12in (30cm) x 0.5mm (SWG 26, AWG 25) bronze wire

- 2 irregular-shaped hollow linking components

- About 70 x 4–5mm random beads, pearls, stone chips and crystals

- 2 x ½–¾in (1 x 2cm) gearwheels

- 2 split-pin fasteners (or rivets)

- Tiny fairy charm

- Nail varnish or enamel paint

- 3 bronze headpins

- 2 glass flowers and 1 glass leaf

- 20in (50cm) tiger-tail beading wire, such as Soft Flex

- Toggle clasp

- 2 necklace end crimps suitable for your beading wire

- Tiny key charm

- 2 x 5in (2cm) lengths of chain

- 11 x 5mm bronze jumprings

❖ EQUIPMENT

- Cutting pliers
- Round-nose pliers
- Superfine-grade sandpaper
- Flat-nose pliers
- Bead stopper (optional)

1 Take the length of wire and wrap it a few times around the edge of your irregular-shaped connector. If you cannot find a connector, you can make your own from a few loops of thick wire, making a wrapped loop at each end, then bending with pliers to an interesting shape.

2 Thread on about 16 of your assorted beads and so on, and wrap the wire around the shape, both horizontally and vertically, filtering the beads a couple at a time to the top of each loop. Keep wrapping until the top view is full of beads. Wrap the wire around one edge a few times and trim.

3 Attach the gearwheels through one of the loops on each wrapped component, using the split pins. If you don't have a split pin, you could rivet them in place.

Mr Dickens suggests...

If this necklace seems very elaborate and you crave something simpler, you could just make the wrapped component piece and hang it as a pendant from a plain chain, threading the chain through a jumpring attached to the gearwheel. Two of the fairy charms and crystal dangles would make wonderful matching earrings.

5 Thread a bead, then a flower onto two of the headpins and make a wrapped loop at the top of each (see page 167). Also make a wrapped loop on the top and bottom of a large bead. Thread a 3in (7.5cm) piece of the wire through the leaf hole, make a loop, then thread the wire end through the hole of the loop at the bottom of the large bead before completing the wrapped loop of the leaf.

4 Use the nail varnish or enamel to add a little colour to the fairy's wings. Leave it to set for at least 24 hours, then gently sand the paint from the raised areas, leaving colour just in the recesses. You could also sand the raised parts of the fairy to add texture and shine (as shown on the top fairy in the image above).

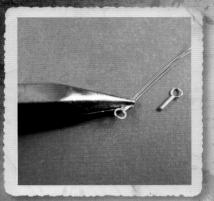

Pages from the Notebook...

Split pins are terribly useful if you can't be bothered to set rivets. You will find them most used in paper crafting, in a variety of styles and finishes including most metals and a rainbow of colours. They come in many different sizes too. I use the tiniest ones most. Do beware of scratching as the split ends can rub against the skin, so make sure they are as flat as can be. Coat them if necessary by dabbing on a bit of two-part epoxy glue and leaving to set.

6 Measure and cut three lengths of beading wire: 2in (5cm), 2½in (6.5cm) and 3¼in (8cm). Thread one end of each length into the end of the necklace, making sure they are arranged in order, and crimp them firmly with the flat-nose pliers.

7 Thread on three colours of beads, one on each thread. I used a very handy gadget called a 'bead stopper' to clamp onto the end of each wire as I finished threading. If you don't have one, you could use a bit of sticky tape. Use the pliers to hold and thread all the ends into the other crimp together, then crimp it shut.

8 Attach the necklace end and rainbow threads to the side of the component that doesn't have a gearwheel with a jumpring. Hang a flower and the tiny key from the loops with jumprings too. Do the same on the other side, but with the flower component and the leaf dangle.

9 Hang the fairy, using a jumpring, from the lowest rainbow length, along with a crystal threaded on a headpin and a loop made at the top. Finally, attach the lengths of chain from each gearwheel with a jumpring. Attach the clasp on the other ends of the chain with the jumprings, giving it a quick rub with the fine sandpaper to reveal the shine on just the raised areas.

FAIRY-WING TIARA

It is a little-known fact that it is perfectly possible to get a good harvest of fairy wings, especially in the very early morning before the dawn light melts them. Fairies are naughty little creatures and love to play chase, pulling each other's hair and wings while squeaking 'Tag!'

As a result of this boisterous activity, the wings often end the night somewhat battered and shabby; these can then be shed and a new pair grown for the following day. The ones you will find lying on the ground are often a little broken or holed, but this can just add to their charm.

Wearing a part of another fairy gives one great power over it, but they are far too lazy to clear up after themselves, relying on dew to dissolve the wings. Queen Mab has made herself a tiara with the discarded wings of her arch enemy Princess Poppycock and takes great delight in wearing it to all the balls and making the princess sit out her favourite dances.

FAIRY-WING TIARA

❖ SUPPLIES

- Small reel of 0.6mm (SWG 24, AWG 23) copper-coloured wire

- Small reel of 0.5mm (SWG 26, AWG 25) copper-coloured wire

- Approximately 6 x 3in (15 x 7.5cm) heat-fusible iridescent film (such as Angelina)

- White craft glue

- Dip It Fantasy Film and hardener

- Gold-coloured tiara band

- Assorted cogs and random beads, pearls and sparkles

- Glitter

❖ EQUIPMENT

- Flat-nose pliers
- Cutting pliers
- Hammer
- Scissors
- Heat gun
- Vinyl/latex gloves
- Piece of polystyrene
- Metal/wooden block

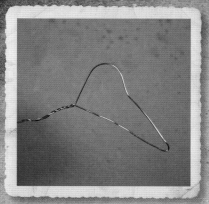

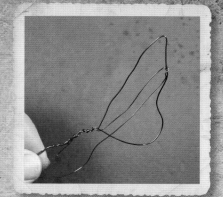

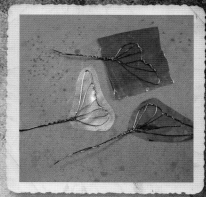

1 Cut a piece of the 0.6mm wire approximately 5in (12cm) long. Use your fingers to bend and curve the wire into a pretty wing shape. Hold the bottom where the wires come together in your pliers and twist the two ends firmly together. Create six or seven more frames, so you can experiment and choose the best.

2 Cut a similar length of 0.5mm wire and wind it a couple of times around the twisted stem of one of the wings to secure. Trace the wire across the wing, wind around the frame and trace it back again to create delicate frame strands. Wind around the frame edge and trim. Hammer gently, just to flatten. Add frame like this to half the wing shapes.

3 Cut pieces of iridescent film off the roll, just a bit bigger than your stranded frames. With your finger, dab a very light coating of glue on one side of the wire frame, press it down onto the film quite firmly and leave to set for at least an hour.

5 Put on the gloves and place your polystyrene block nearby. Take the unstranded wing frames and dip in the Dip It Fantasy Film, following the manufacturer's instructions. Carefully sprinkle glitter on while the film is still wet (it dries very quickly), then place the stems in the polystyrene and leave to dry. When dry, dip again in the clear hardener. Make sure you wear gloves as it can be sticky. Leave the wings to dry overnight.

4 Trim around the wing shape to about ¼in (5mm). Use a heat gun to heat and shrink the film around the frame. Try to manoeuvre the outer film edges as they shrink, so they curve up and over the frame. You will find the colours change and get more iridescent as the film heats. You can also make tiny holes by heating a bit more in one spot.

Mr Woppit suggests...

Look at the shapes of butterfly wings for inspiration for your wire-frame shapes. Simply bend and manipulate them to follow the shapes you like. You can wrap wire around pencils, cotton reels, and all sorts of things to get nice even shapes if you're not confident going free-hand.

6 To create the other components, cut pieces of 0.5mm wire approximately 8in (20cm) long. Thread halfway through a handy hole in the assorted cogs and beads, bend and twist tightly to secure. The neatest twist comes from holding the two wires firmly and twisting the object.

Pages from the Notebook...

Dip It Fantasy Film can get thick and gloopy, so you may need the matching thinner. If it seems the wrong consistency, add the thinner a little at a time until it gives a light and airy film. It takes a bit of practice, so do make extra wings. If it goes wrong, you can melt it off by simply redipping in the pot.

8 Place the next component along and tightly wrap the wire to hold that piece down too. Work your way around one side of the tiara, trim the wire, return to the middle and add the components on the other side one at a time in the same manner.

7 Lay the main components out in front of you and arrange them as you wish them to be grouped. Make a right-angle bend in each wire at the height you want them to sit, half going right, half left, and trim to 2in (5cm). Cut a length of 0.5mm wire approximately 15in (37.5cm) long and wrap tightly in the centre of the tiara band. Place the first component with its wire behind the band, and wrap the attached wire twice tightly near the bend in the component wire.

9 Cut another 15in (37.5cm) piece of 0.5mm wire and secure by wrapping at the edge of the furthest wire strand. Thread on some beads and crystals. Wind this wire around the band, between the components, positioning a bead or several small beads always to the front of the band. This covers any messy wire and adds more texture and sparkle. Add more wire if necessary, wrap tightly a few times to finish and trim closely.

F. DAVEY

28 St. Ildate St. Gloucester.

KRAKEN RIDER

As we walked along the moonlit beach, I noticed the waves seemed to be rolling backwards. Instead of crashing in wonderful breakers, the foam was drawn backwards into waves far out at sea. I commented upon this to the Admiral and he sighed.

He had offended a sea sprite (quite how I did not think it polite to enquire), and in retaliation she had turned all his ordered, nautical world topsy-turvy. Now the waves roll the wrong way, birds fly underwater and fish swim in the air. The figurehead on the prow of the ship inspires them onwards, suggesting compass bearings to the steersman as she rides the waves, and this will continue until he fulfils three tasks.

The three tasks didn't seem that difficult to me, to be honest – opening the giant oyster to gain the pearl was merely a matter of levers and pulleys, while defeating the Kraken would have been the work of a moment for my monster-hunting friends. The gathering of the moon's reflection, however, seemed a little trickier, so I promised the Admiral to give it some thought.

'ADVENTURES FIRST, EXPLANATIONS AFTER' CRAVAT

'I could not agree more,' said Emilly when catching sight of Lord Davey's cravat. 'However, as we seem to have had quite an adventure already, perhaps now might be a good time to start the explanation?'

Spirits remained high upon the raft, despite the heavy rain and sporadic shark-fin sighting. The occasional flash of bright lightning lit up the sky and spread luminescent trickles across the waves.

St Elmo's fire lit up the prow of the ship, proudly silhouetted at an improbable angle against the sky, and the wrecked engine bobbed past, sadly reduced to an assortment of gearwheels and unusual steam mechanisms. Apparently the engine at least was unsinkable…

'ADVENTURES FIRST, EXPLANATIONS AFTER' CRAVAT

❖ SUPPLIES

- Images for transfer (similar to the one opposite) saved on computer as JPEGs at 300dpi

- 20in (50cm) pale-coloured silk taffeta

- StazOn inkpad

- Kitchen parchment paper

- Iron-on fabric-printing transfer paper (either for inkjet or laser depending on your printer)

❖ EQUIPMENT

- Printer (inkjet or laser)
- Iron
- Rubber stamp
- Sewing machine

Use this image as inspiration for your own.

Adventures first!

Explanations take such a dreadful time

Explanations take such a dreadful time

Adventures first!

1 Choose or create your images with a drawing or painting computer program such as Photoshop or Illustrator. Remember you can use only images that are copyright-free or 'creative commons' or your own artwork. Leave plenty of pale or white areas in your images; these can be overprinted with the rubber stamp later. Flip the image so it will print in reverse with 'mirror writing'. See the artwork on page 45 for inspiration.

2 Draw the pattern on a large piece of paper (see page 49), cut it out and lay it onto your folded fabric, placing the 'fold' mark against the fabric fold. Cut out two identical shapes; one for the front, which will be decorated, and one for the lining, which will remain plain.

3 Print out your images onto the transfer paper, being careful to load the paper sheets one at a time the right way up. Cut out the images. Following the manufacturer's instructions carefully for your brand of paper, place the images pleasingly on the unfolded front fabric and iron them in place, peeling the paper away afterwards.

5 Place the decorated piece on top of the lining, with the decorated side down. Starting in the middle of one of the long sides, pin, and then sew, all around the outside with a ½in (1cm) hem, leaving a 2in (5cm) gap. Clip the corners and turn the right way out through the little gap you left. Iron flat, placing parchment paper under the images as before – never let your iron touch the images.

4 Use the rubber stamp and inkpad to print more interesting shapes and texture details on the pale image areas. Try hard not to move the stamp as you print or it will blur. Placing the fabric on a pile of newspapers or magazines will give it a little cushion to aid neat stamping. Allow to dry completely, then iron quickly to seal, placing a piece of kitchen parchment paper over the image to protect your iron.

Pages from the Notebook…

There are many types of iron-on backing for ironing onto dark fabrics. Some work almost like a dye, leaving no shiny glue layer at all. There are also specific types for inkjet and laser printers or photocopiers. Choose the one that works best for you. It's always worth doing a test print on a bit of your chosen fabric to make sure you have the transfer technique correct. Always read the instructions for your specific paper before you start.

Mr Dickens advises...

You can create a matching handkerchief using the techniques you've learned. Cut a handkerchief-sized piece of silk, iron a very narrow hem on all edges, then sew. Finally add your decorations. This method of fabric decoration is suitable only for items that won't be washed much; you could design your own fabric and get it printed on washable cotton instead. You can buy fabric printed with your own designs at www.spoonflower.com.

6 Fold the cravat in half lengthways and mark the centre, then create four small tucks down the length of the cravat through both layers of material. Secure each tuck for around 10in (25cm) with pins. Stitch them down with five lines across the narrow width, one in the very centre, and the others 3in (7.5cm) and 5in (12.5cm) either side of the centre point. Remove the pins and press the tucks between stitches to neaten.

❖ **PATTERN**   Draw the shape on a large piece of paper (newspaper will do) using the sizes indicated and cut out.

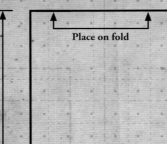

Place on fold

6in (15cm)

42in (107cm)

Cut one lining and one outer

1½in (4cm)

KRAKEN RING

The kraken and its thrashing tentacles is one of the most feared objects in the sea. Seeking out, then holding fast in its grip any object, from a swift tea clipper to a mermaid's comb, it has a reputation for destruction. But some ocean kraken have befriended becalmed vessels or shipwrecked mariners, gently pushing them towards the shore.

The island colony of Hy-Brasil is one such place, founded by the crew of a small vessel, rescued by a kraken that took a fancy to the ship's cat. Wrapping a tentacle gently around the cat, the kraken kept it out of the salt water for the eight days it took to push the wreckage to the mysterious isle, inhabited only by black rabbits.

KRAKEN RING

❖ SUPPLIES

- 2oz (50g) packet of black polymer clay

- Scrap of grey polymer clay

- Liquid polymer clay

- Copper-coloured acrylic paint, such as Swellegant! base coat

- Patina solution in verdigris

- Indigo dye

- Compatible varnish or proprietary sealant

❖ EQUIPMENT

- Paper ring gauges
- Ring mandrel
- Craft knife
- Cocktail stick
- Modelling tools
- Paintbrush

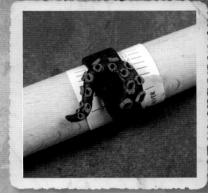

1 Condition the black polymer clay by rolling and kneading it between your fingers until soft and pliable. Roll out a piece long and wide enough to go around your finger – approximately 1/16in (2mm) thick and 1/3in (8mm) wide. Wrap the paper ring gauge around the mandrel to your correct ring size and secure. Place the clay strip around the paper. Where it overlaps, cut at an angle through both layers. Use a tiny amount of liquid clay to secure and bake for 5 minutes at the temperature recommended by your clay's manufacturer.

2 Roll out two sausage shapes from the black polymer clay, about 2in (5cm) long and 1/4in (5mm) thick. Taper them at one end, to form a rounded point. Roll another piece of scrap clay to form a sausage 1/16in (2mm) wide. Cut off tiny pieces of the clay with the craft knife and press into the tentacle shape in pairs to form suckers. Make a small hole in the middle of each piece using a cocktail stick.

3 Use a slightly larger round modelling tool to form the centre of the suckers into tiny circles. Take one tentacle and cut the wide end at an angle. Paint the underside with liquid clay and position on the ring where the join is. Gently curve it into a sinuous shape, pressing with your modelling tool inside the suckers to stick it firmly to the ring. Bake for 5 minutes and allow to cool.

4 Attach the second tentacle in the same way, positioning the angled cut on the ring and then swirling in the opposite direction to the first one. Use a cocktail stick to press it down to secure. It needs to feel reasonably firm, but the liquid clay will bake a very solid bond. Bake the whole ring for 20 minutes this time and allow to cool thoroughly.

Pages from the Notebook...

If your clay begins to become too malleable or sticky while sculpting, put it somewhere cool for a few hours. This is particularly useful when cutting out suckers from the thin strip of clay. After rolling out the thin sausage, leave it to rest so that it won't change shape as you cut it. Another tip is to gently push away from you as you cut, with a very sharp scalpel, so the sausage turns as you slice. This also helps to cut a nice, crisp circle.

6 Paint the clay with the copper base coat again. While it is still wet, dab or drip the verdigris patina solution over it. Leave to dry and let the patina develop. Add a wash of indigo dye (or watered down acrylic paint if you are using acrylics), then dry brush a little of the original copper colour onto the highlights. When it is completely dry, paint with compatible varnish or proprietary sealant.

5 Completely cover the ring in copper Swellegant! base coat or acrylic paint. Get into all the little cracks. You don't have to do the inside of the ring, but do be sure to do the top and bottom. Leave to dry thoroughly. If using paint, add another coat and leave to dry.

PORTHOLE BRACELET

Many leagues down into the dark waters beneath the pale sun, strange creatures swim and dive. Sometimes only the merest hint of a tentacle may be seen emerging from the gloom; sometimes a strange species glides past, apparently unaware of any observer.

The viewing gallery aboard The Spirula is luxurious in the extreme. Lush, aquamarine velvet chaise longues are grouped around each porthole and carved gilt seashells adorn every surface. No expense was spared in its outfitting and all the very latest in mechanical outfitting was employed by The Mauve Star Line. However, it is rather a shame that this aura of extreme gentility and good taste is somewhat spoiled by a pianola that can play only, 'Oh I do like to be beside the seaside'.

PORTHOLE BRACELET

❖ SUPPLIES

- An image 10½ x 3½in (27 x 9cm), similar to that shown on the opposite page; you can draw it yourself or maybe use wrapping paper

- A4 sheet of Grafix Inkjet Printable Shrink Film in Matte

- Tim Holtz Distress Ink pad in Vintage Photo (optional)

- Tissue or sponge

- 2in (5cm) deep brass cuff blank

- 4 x 7mm x 3.5mm nail head rivets

- 2 plated portholes (size to match pattern)

- Metal octopus charm

- 2-part epoxy glue

- 2-part epoxy paste

- Adhesive putty

❖ EQUIPMENT

- Scissors
- Craft knife
- Cutting mat
- Heat gun/oven
- Dremel drill/metal hole punch
- Round file
- Flat file
- Eye protectors
- Cutting pliers
- Hammer and rivet-setting block
- Plastic-covered pliers or wooden mandrel
- Modelling tool
- Cocktail stick

1 Print your image onto the shrink plastic film, testing on normal paper first. You will need an image about 10½ x 3½in (27 x 9cm), which will eventually shrink down to about 5 x 1½in (13 x 4cm). You can copy the one below or create your own. If you use your own, don't forget to mark some appropriately sized spaces for the portholes, and remember the colours will intensify dramatically when the plastic shrinks, so keep them pale and clear, with an opacity of about 50 per cent.

2 Cut out the printed piece with scissors, rounding the corners. Cut out the porthole areas carefully with a craft knife – shrink plastic is quite tough so use a cutting mat and score a few times, gradually cutting deeper.

3 If you like, you can use Distress Ink to age the edges of the plastic. Apply in a circular motion with a tissue or sponge, just on the corners and edges and around the porthole spaces for an added vintage feel.

5 Drill four holes with your drill or hole punch, in the corners of the shrink plastic piece. Place a piece of wood on your bench as a base and drill down into it through the plastic – it shouldn't need much pressure. The drill bit should be the same size as the stem of your rivets. If the plastic melts onto the drill bit, just wait a moment until it cools and then peel it off. Neaten the holes if necessary with a round file.

4 Shrink the plastic according to the manufacturer's instructions. For larger pieces I like to use the oven as it gives a good even shrink, but it only takes 30 seconds to a minute so keep an eye on it. While it is still warm, drape it over the cuff blank and let it set into the correct shape on the form. If you don't have an oven to hand, then a heat gun can be used – just keep it moving so as not to burn or distort the piece as it shrinks.

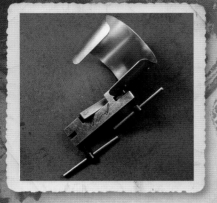

6 Place the plastic over the cuff blank and mark where the holes are. Drill or pierce with a hole-cutting tool in these places, and neaten with a file if necessary. Always wear eye protection when drilling metal.

Pages from the Notebook...

Different types of shrink plastic shrink different amounts, so if you are using a different brand to the one that I used, it is a good idea to shrink a test piece first to see what percentage it shrinks by. Just mark out a 2in (5cm) square and measure it again after shrinking. Divide the difference in size by the original size and multiply by 100 to get the percentage the plastic has shrunk by.

This is a good way of checking the colouring too, as it allows you to adjust the intensity of the print.

7 Place the plastic over the metal and thread the rivets through both layers, from the front of the piece. Working on the inside of the cuff, trim the stems with pliers to within ¹⁄₁₆in (2mm) and flat file them till they are a nice flat shape. Using a hammer and rivet-setting block, gently tap all around the edge of the wire stem, creating a little mushroom shape. It is quite hard to set a rivet on the inside of the piece, but little taps will get it done eventually.

8 Curve the plated portholes and the octopus into shape using plastic-covered pliers, wooden mandrels or a hammer – whatever you are most comfortable with. Keep 'offering up' the shapes to where they will finally sit and check they lie nicely on the curve of the bracelet. It's worth taking your time over this to get it looking right.

Mr Rivett suggests...

Practise setting rivets flat before trying curved surfaces. If you find this type of rivet is just too much trouble, you can also find two-part ones with a front and back piece that slot together. Another idea would be to drill a larger hole and set an eyelet through instead of a rivet, or even use a split paper fastener.

9 Mix up some 2-part epoxy glue and attach the portholes using a cocktail stick. Place in position and use a bit of adhesive putty over the top, just to hold them if they look like they might slip due to the curve. Mix up some 2-part epoxy paste and fill the back of the octopus with it, then place on the cuff and press firmly. Use a modelling tool to remove any oozed paste. Leave to set for at least 12 hours.

MERMAID EARRINGS

Despite rather sad stories about unrequited love, mermaids remain a popular attraction for tourists in the misty regions surrounding the Isles of Sky. They can be admired leaping through the waves, their tails and fins an assortment of blue, green and violet hues.

A popular trip for lovers is aboard a hover platform, which floats above the waves, providing a smooth and gentle ride out to where the creatures play in the bay. Many a young gentleman has attempted to pop the question while his paramour was otherwise distracted by the antics of the pretty fish people.

MERMAID EARRINGS

❖ SUPPLIES

- 2 brass-coloured mermaid charms

- 2 x ½in (1cm) brass gearwheels

- 2 brass-coloured headpins

- Very strong beading thread, such as Nymo

- Approximately 1g each of 3 different-coloured size 10 seed beads

- 6 assorted chains of 2in (5cm) length

- 4 x 6mm different-coloured jumprings

- 2 brass-coloured earring hooks

❖ EQUIPMENT

- Round-nose pliers
- Beading needle
- Scissors
- Flat-nose pliers

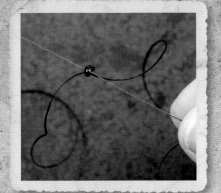

1 Thread a headpin through the top of one of the mermaids and the centre of a brass gearwheel behind. Snip off the tail of the pin to about 1in (2.5cm). Grip tightly at the tip with round-nose pliers, then roll up in a spiral until the cog is firmly held against the mermaid.

2 Thread the beading needle with approximately 15in (36cm) of strong beading thread and pass the needle through and around a seed bead, in a loop; do this a few times to create a stopper bead. Leave a tail of about 2–3in (5–7.5cm).

3 Thread on about 12 more seed beads. Use the bottom bead as a turning bead and pass the needle up through the next five beads in the opposite direction to the way you threaded them on.

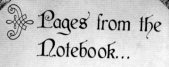

Pages from the Notebook...

There are many types of beading thread and needles. The easiest for bead weaving is a stiff, sharp needle, which needs to be very fine to pass up and down the same beads several times. Nymo is a very strong type of beading thread, which is very thin and fine so it doesn't block the holes of the beads.

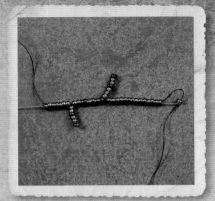

4 Thread on around 15 more seeds, once more use the bottom bead as a turning bead and pass the needle up through five beads.

5 Make a final branch in the same way. On the final branch, pass the needle all the way up to the top of the stem, bypassing the other branches. Pull until firm but not too tight or it will not hang correctly.

6 Add on eight seed beads and loop through the hole in the mermaid's tail, passing the needle back down through the stopper bead and the two beads below it.

Mr Rivett suggests...

You can add patina to the tail of the mermaid before you start making the earrings to give it extra depth and colour – use your favourite method. After you've added the colour, lightly sand with a superfine sanding pad to reveal the raised metal areas.

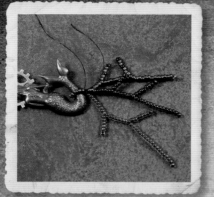

8 Thread one piece of chain onto one jump ring and two pieces of chain to the other. Close the rings around the mermaid's tail either side of the seaweed strands.

7 Create a second and third strand of seaweed, following steps 3–6 and passing the thread through the same loop of beads on the mermaid's tail each time. Tie a knot with the end of the thread and the piece of thread next to the stopper bead; pass each thread through a few beads and trim.

9 Gently twist the earring hook loop open and thread on the cog. Twist closed once more. Repeat the whole process for the other earring.

J.E. Reeves

50. HERMIT ROAD,
CANNING TOWN

BROKEN DOLLS' PICNIC

*I was gasping for a cup of tea and a slice of cake when
Mr Woppit and I happened upon a beautiful rose garden filled
with the sound of delicate china cups being filled and glasses
clinking. Hanging from the rose bushes were tiny Chinese lanterns
of every colour, each one glowing gently in the twilight.*

I noticed a family of teddy bears, somewhat 'well loved' – one was
missing an ear, another had very little fur left – tucking into
a large honey cake with gusto. A rather battered selection
of soldiers was exchanging war stories under a pergola as they
raised glasses to toast some pretty, though shabby, dolls.

And oh how the tea table was piled with glorious confections! It made
my mouth water to look. As a glass was pressed into one of my hands
and a plate into the other, I felt a tightening in my joints and my legs
didn't seem to bend quite as they used to. I ignored these peculiar
sensations and picked up a large purple meringue oozing with cream.
I was just about to take a bite when a cuddly toy rabbit barged at me
and knocked me quite off my feet and out of the rose garden.

'DRINK ME' BRACELET

It is not often a good idea to consume bottles of coloured liquid with no other label than, 'Drink me'. However, it had been a very long day, and after wandering around the wood for what seemed like hours, Emilly was more than ready for a cocktail or two. She carefully poured each one into a small glass and gave it a stir with a handy cherry.

'In the absence of tea, you'll just have to do! Splashy splashy,' said Emilly.

Gentle reader, we shall draw a veil over the following three hours and the very peculiar things that happened. Let us just say that sometimes Emilly sighs for the emerald-green hair, though Mr Woppit is then quick to point out that purple eyes are all very well, but leaving a trail of stars wherever you go is just showing off.

'DRINK ME' BRACELET

❖ SUPPLIES

- 5 little vials

- Coloured liquids (cordials, syrups and liqueurs)

- Metal-effect paint, such as Viva Decor Ferro in Iron

- Alcohol ink

- A4 sheet of matt shrink plastic

- Tim Holtz Distress Ink pad in Vintage Photo

- About 15 x 5mm etched jumprings

- Key and pocket watch loop and toggle clasp

- Heavy copper-coloured bracelet chain approximately 8in (20cm) long (adjust for your wrist as necessary)

- About 10 copper-coloured headpins

- About 10 assorted beads and pearls

- 4 key and lock charms

- About 10 x 8mm etched jumprings

- 2-part epoxy glue

- Cotton wool

❖ EQUIPMENT

- Syringe
- Cocktail stick
- Label-shaped hole punch
- Scissors
- Rubber stamp
- Permanent marker pen
- Heat gun
- Round-nose pliers
- Cutting pliers
- Flat-nose pliers

1 To fill the vials, draw one of the coloured liquids up into the syringe. Gently drip the required amount of liquid into the vial and seal it with the supplied rubber bung. Dry the top of the vial thoroughly. Mix up some 2-part epoxy glue and dab it over the top and neck of the vial. Place the metal lid on the vial and let the glue set. Repeat for the other vials.

2 To give the vials a rusty, aged effect, use a cocktail stick to press on some metal-effect paint where the glass meets the lid and in places on the metal too. Add a few drops of alcohol ink to colour the silver and blend the metal with the metal-effect paint. There's no need for a brush – just drop it straight from the bottle! Leave to dry.

3 Cut out four label shapes about 1 x 1½in (2.5 x 4cm) from the shrink plastic. Punch out a large hole for attaching the label. Dab the cotton wool onto the stamp pad and, using a circular motion, add a light coating of ink to the edges of the labels and around the hole. Use the rubber stamp and stamp pad to add detail around the hole. Write 'Drink Me!' on the label using a permanent marker pen.

Mr Rivett suggests...

If you prefer a more graphic-design approach rather than handwriting and stamping, why not print out teeny labels onto printable shrink plastic, cut out, punch a hole and shrink as instructed. Remember that the colours will intensify considerably, so adjust the print colours to pastel versions by reducing the opacity.

Pages from the Notebook...

Add glitter or glow-in-the-dark powder to give extra sparkles to the coloured liquids. Simply drop a pinch in before you add the liquid. It's also great fun to make interesting loops and toggles from found objects such as washers and twisted wire.

4 Place a label on a heatproof surface and gently hold it down with a long-handled metal implement. Use a heat gun to gently heat the label until it starts to distort. Keep heating it until it has fully shrunk and flattened out. While it's still warm you can twist it to achieve a 'paper blown past on the wind' feel. If it goes too hard, just heat again. Repeat with the other labels.

5 Use 5mm jumprings to attach the loop and toggle clasp to the chain. Check it is the right size for your wrist and that you can do it up easily. Add or take off chain loops as necessary, using the pliers. I also slightly flattened the top of my key toggle into an oval shape with flat-nose pliers, so it would fit through the pocket-watch loop.

6 Thread the beads onto the headpins and create wrapped loops at the top (see page 167), then trim neatly. Starting at the centre of the chain, attach a vial, then attach your charms, vials and labels using assorted sized jumprings. Try to keep a fairly even pattern on each side, sometimes placing more than one bead or charm on a chain loop.

LOLLIPOP CRAVAT PIN

The stripy stocking tree is a rare and wondrous piece of botanical history. Presented to Lord Benedict Barley Sugar by a grateful guild of sugar spinners as a potential symbol of his family business, its branches grow into the most extraordinary likenesses of banded socks.

Cuttings have been taken from the tree, and bred into a variety of hues and patterns. Fancy bandings are considered particularly desirable and it is now quite the fashion to sport walking sticks, and other decorative accessories, made from the wood.

Care must be taken, however, when effecting realistic carving of similarly coloured sweets. Much embarrassment could have been avoided at the theatre, if only Lord Barley Sugar had kept his whittling separate from Milady's humbugs.

LOLLIPOP CRAVAT PIN

❖ SUPPLIES

• 2-part epoxy resin, rectangular moulds, vinyl gloves and wooden stirrer

• Assorted tiny cogs and gearwheels

• Coloured paper or a picture

• Tim Holtz Distress Ink pad in Vintage Photo

• Tissue or sponge

• Stick pin back and cap end

• Sticky tape, PVA glue or Golden Gel Medium in Gloss

• Adhesive putty (optional)

❖ EQUIPMENT

• Paper ring gauges
• Ring mandrel
• Craft knife
• Cocktail stick
• Modelling tools
• Paintbrush

2 Place a cog or tiny watch part in the corner of the mould shape. Mix up another batch of resin and gently pour over the cog to about ⅟₁₆in (2mm) depth in the mould. If the cog moves, rearrange it using a cocktail or lollipop stick. Leave to set as before.

1 Using the vinyl gloves and wooden stirrer, mix up about 1fl oz (30ml) of resin in the disposable cup. Follow the manufacturer's instructions carefully, as different resins will mix in different ratios of hardener to resin. Mix thoroughly, stirring for about 5 minutes, but you don't need to beat it and make it frothy! Tap the cup hard on the table to help the bubbles rise to the surface. Pour a very thin layer onto the base of each rectangle in the mould and spread to the edges. It should be about ⅟₃₂in (1mm) thick. Cover the mould with a bit of paper and leave to set somewhere dry and free from dust for about 12 hours.

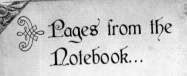

Pages from the Notebook…

If your resin doesn't set, either the proportions were wrong or it was insufficiently mixed. All is not lost, however. If you carefully mix up another batch and pour it over, it will set on top of the unset, rubbery one, providing a hard shell, and the rubbery one may set eventually underneath.

If you touch it too soon and get thumb marks on the resin, wait until it is fully cured, then you can polish them off using extremely fine sanding or polishing cloths. If it is a deep scratch, you can paint a layer of resin on all over, which will fill the scratch.

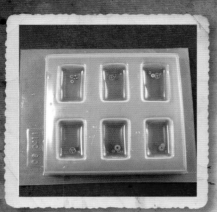

3 Add more cogs, overlapping the previous layer so they will appear to be floating behind each other, then pour the resin in and leave to set as before. Add a third layer of cogs, watch hands and resin to create a dense, interesting composition of floating watch parts.

4 Cut out your background from the coloured paper or picture to the right size and shape to fit the mould nicely. Distress the edges of the paper using the Distress Ink pad; dab some ink in a circular motion on the edges and corners, using a tissue or sponge. Encapsulate the image with a piece of sticky tape or PVA glue, and trim leaving a tiny border (see Useful Advice box, left).

USEFUL ADVICE

If you don't encapsulate your image properly, the resin will seep in and turn the paper transparent. To use sticky tape, stick two pieces either side of the image, press very firmly and trim with a $\frac{1}{16}$in (2mm) border. To use Golden Gel Medium, spread a thin layer on a plastic surface, place the image face down, then spread more medium on the top. Leave until completely dry (12 hours), peel off and trim with a border as before. To use PVA glue, simply paint the glue on one side, leave to dry, paint the other, then seal all the edges very thoroughly.

5 Place the image face down in the mould and press firmly all over with the end of a paintbrush or similar. Mix up a final batch of resin and pour in over the back of the image. Position the stick pin, using a mound of adhesive putty on the side of the mould to hold it in place while it dries if necessary.

6 Once the resin is set, gently ease your cravat pins out of the moulds.

TOPIARY PENDANT

The noble art of topiary has been introduced to the area by the Marchioness of Marqueyssac, a delicate doll who was lost, along with a small sewing basket, among the scented rosebushes long ago. She snips the shrubs into glorious and fantastical forms with her specially designed steam scissors.

When she deems the temperature is correct, she simply uses the boiling water for a fragrant cup of Rose Pouchong tea and pauses to admire her handiwork. So realistic are her sculptures that White Rabbit spent a good half-hour trying to work out how to detach the topiary dirigible from its moorings.

TOPIARY PENDANT

❖ SUPPLIES

- Brass rod of 1/16in (2mm) diameter

- Small pieces of green polymer clay in three shades

- Interesting large-toothed cog aprox 1¼in (3cm)

- 2-part silicone modelling compound

- Gold polymer clay

- ¼ pack green polymer clay

- Liquid polymer clay

- 2in (5cm) of 0.6mm (SWG 24, AWG 23) copper-coloured wire

- Alcohol ink (ginger colour)

- 2-part epoxy resin

- Resin dye or oil paint (light brown)

- Tiny dolls' house cup and saucer

- Glue

❖ EQUIPMENT

- Small fret saw
- Flat file
- Coarse cheese grater
- Paintbrush
- Pasta machine (optional)
- 1in (2.5cm) round cutter
- ¾in (2cm) fancy-shaped cutter
- Cocktail stick
- Superfine-grade sandpaper
- Drill

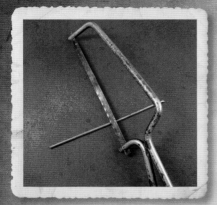

1 Cut the brass rod into a 2in (5cm) length using a small fret saw. File off any rough edges. If you don't have a brass rod, you could use a cocktail stick painted gold with acrylic paint instead. Just snip off the pointed ends and sandpaper smooth before painting.

2 Condition hazelnut-sized pieces of the three shades of green polymer clay by rolling and kneading them between your fingers until soft and pliable. Roll into balls, and bake at the manufacturer's recommended temperature for 5–7 minutes. When cool, grate finely, mix and set aside.

3 Make a mould of your cog using 2-part silicone compound. Take equal amounts of each part and knead them together. Place your cog on a flat surface, fancy side up, and press the compound over it. Leave to set for at least an hour. Press conditioned gold clay into your mould to make two cogs.

4 Condition and roll out the main block of green clay. I used a pasta machine set to approximately ¹⁄₁₆in (2mm) thickness. Cut out two top-hat shapes and two circles.

5 Place a little bobble of clay on the tip of the brass rod; make sure it's well anchored to the metal. Sandwich it between the two top-hat shapes. Repeat for the cog shapes a little further down the rod and then do the same for the circles near the bottom of the rod.

6 Make a small wrapped loop from the wire (see page 166). Trim the end to ¼in (5mm), then curve the cut end into a hook with round-nose pliers and insert into the top of the hat shape. Smooth the clay round the edges with a cocktail stick to give a good join. Bake for 5 minutes at the recommended temperature.

USEFUL ADVICE

Use epoxy resin to glue the saucer to the cup and also any loose bits of topiary onto the brass pole. Remember that resin will not withstand heat, so do this at the end.

You could also make it into a pin by omitting the hanging loop and gluing a finding to the back of one of the topiary balls instead. To design your own tiny shapes for the top, like my top hat, fold a piece of paper in half, draw and cut out half the shape, then use a scalpel to cut out identical shapes in polymer with the paper as a template.

7 When cool, brush one side of the green circle and the hat shape with a thick coat of liquid polymer clay. Sprinkle the grated green clay mix over thickly, give it a moment to stick, then pick the piece up, holding it over a piece of paper so any excess just falls off. Bake for 5 minutes, textured side upwards, then allow to cool. Repeat the process for the other side, and also for the edges.

Pages from the Notebook...

Although it may seem very time-consuming to have to let the resin in the tea cup set before drilling a hole in it, this is the best way to ensure that your topiary stands upright. If you just stick the tree into wet resin you will find it will be very difficult to keep it in an upright position while the resin dries. An alternative way of doing it would be to use resin paste instead and just wedge the stem into the thick paste while it dries.

8 Brush the alcohol ink onto both sides and edges of the cog shape and allow to dry. Gently sand off the ink on the raised areas with superfine-grade sandpaper to give the piece texture and patina. Work your way up through the grades of paper to get a smooth metallic shine.

9 Mix up a tiny amount of 2-part epoxy resin and add resin dye or oil paint to make it look like tea. Pour it into the little cup and leave to set. When set, drill a hole the same width as the brass rod, pop a tiny bit of glue on the tip of the rod and insert the topiary into the hole.

MINI TOP HAT

When taking afternoon tea with the toys, correct attire is very
important. Ladies must wear a hat, no matter how tiny or extravagant.
As for gentlemen, their swords should never be brought to table.

This can be problematic for the steadfast tin soldier, whose sword is
welded on, sadly, but the paper ballerina takes him his own cup and
they sit in the shade of the willow and talk, hand in hand.

Some clever dolls have trained beautiful birds to perch on the
brims of their hats as decorations, spreading their feathers
or chiming sweet notes on the hour.

Mechanical butterflies and novelty automata are also
popular additions to the millinery, though it can be startling
to have a neighbour's jack-in-the-box leap out unexpectedly,
especially when one has a mouthful of tea.

MINI TOP HAT

❖ SUPPLIES

- 20in (50cm) buckram

- 20in (50cm) felt fabric or compressed volume fleece (this layer is called the 'mull')

- 20in (50cm) purple and red shot silk outer fabric

- 10in (25cm) lining fabric

- Hot glue sticks

- Matching sewing thread

- 20in (50cm) bias binding (shop-bought or homemade to match your fabric)

- All-purpose fabric glue

- Trims, ribbons, feathers, old watch parts etc

- Approximately 15in (37.5cm) narrow (¼in/5mm) elastic in a similar colour to your hair

❖ EQUIPMENT

- Pattern paper or a photocopier
- Fabric and paper scissors
- Chalk pencil for fabric and pen
- Glue gun
- Hand-sewing needles and pins
- Sewing machine
- Iron
- Craft knife/scalpel

1 Photocopy the pattern (page 103) at 200 per cent or scale the pattern up to twice the size on pattern paper. Cut the pattern out and lay it on the buckram first. Draw around the pattern, leaving no seam allowance except for a 1in (2.5cm) overlap on the centre back. Cut out the buckram, but do not cut the inside circle of the brim. Next draw around the pattern on the mull and cut out, leaving a 1in (2.5cm) seam allowance on every cut edge. On the main fabric and linings, draw around the pattern with a chalk fabric pencil. Remember to take into account the grain lines on the outer fabric and leave 1in (2.5cm) seam allowances on both.

2 Put the glue gun on to heat up, and curve the buckram of the crown side piece around into the correct shape, noting where it overlaps at the back with the 1in (2.5cm) seam allowance. Put plenty of hot glue on the overlap and immediately press the other edge over it, matching the centre back line. Glue the crown's tip on using hot glue also, working from the inside of the hat. When cool, place fabric glue over the corresponding felt crown side piece and wrap it around the hat. Squeeze the felt overlap together at the centre back and trim it flush. When the glue is dry, trim the excess felt top and bottom.

3 Glue the felt crown tip on also and trim when dry to make a neat shape. Take the crown tip fabric piece and pin it to the hat all around with pins placed vertically through the felt only; don't try to push them through the buckram. Sew the fabric down to the mull only with a neat running stitch ¼in (0.5cm) from the top edge. Snip and trim the fabric if necessary to get a nice, flat, even finish. Remove the pins. Smooth the bottom edge of the fabric up inside the crown like a hem, and sew down through the buckram and mull, with a running stitch again.

5 Glue the felt pieces down onto both sides of the brim piece using the fabric glue. When the glue is dry, trim the edges neatly all around the outside. Mark the central hole shape with a pen on the felt, and also the front and back marking. Hand tack one piece of the brim fabric down onto the felt.

4 Wrap the crown side fabric around the crown inside out. Make sure there is 1in (2.5cm) of fabric above and below the solid shape all the way around, and pin down the centre back. Slide the shape out and sew the seam, either with a machine or by hand. Press the seam open and also press under the 1in (2.5cm) allowance on the top edge. Put the fabric right side out on the form over the raw edges of the crown tip, and invisible slipstitch all the way around on the top edge.

USEFUL ADVICE

If you don't feel your sewing skills are up to the full traditional construction, or you just need a quick, fancy-dress hat, why not use the pattern to make a hat from coloured card and decorate it with paper flowers? You could attach this sort of hat to an Alice band rather than elastic, to make it easy to wear.

Mini hats always look best worn at a jaunty angle, forward and to one side of the head, like a fascinator, and this will help keep the hat on too. If your hat slips, you probably don't have it far enough forward.

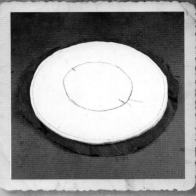

6 Using the drawn line as a guide, machine stitch around the inside brim hole shape, keeping the felt side uppermost and the fabric side down on the machine bed. Also stitch around the edge about ¼in (5mm) from the trimmed fabric. Tack the second piece of fabric to the remaining felt side and, turning the brim over, sew again, following along the existing machine stitches. Buckram is tough, so you will want a sharp, heavy-duty needle.

7 Attach bias binding all around the edge of the brim. I like to machine sew one edge, then fold the binding around the edge and hand slipstitch the other side, but you can hand stitch both sides or machine stitch it all, depending on your preferred technique. If you like, you can steam the brim into a curved shape using an iron or a kettle; once the brim is soft, curve it into shape and hold until it hardens. Cut the central hole into a star shape using a craft knife to start the cuts, then scissors if it's easier. Trim some of the fabric down a little and curve the petals up ready to hot glue to the inside of the crown.

Pages from the Notebook...

There are a few tips that will give you a lovely professional finish to your hat. When attaching bias binding, don't forget to fold in the end as you begin, so as to get a lovely neat finish on the join. Do take your time when you are gluing and sewing. Keep your stitches neat and even and be very careful with glue, as it will mark any fabric you accidentally get it on.

Remember, hot glue is hot, so keep a cup of cold water next to you to dip your fingers into if you touch it. I suggest using a low-melt glue gun rather than a super-hot one as it does just as good a job.

8 Put a good dollop of hot glue on the inside of a cut brim petal and press it firmly into the correct place inside the crown, matching the centre back and front. Hold until it is set, and then do the next one. When the hat is glued together, add your decorations, either by gluing in place or by firmly sewing right through the buckram.

9 Try on the hat and measure your elastic length. Glue the elastic in place slightly towards the front of the hat, so the tension will keep it on your head nicely. Cut out the lining shapes for the crown only with a 1in (2.5cm) seam allowance, then mark the actual shape in chalk on the fabric. Sew up the back seam of the crown side lining first, then pin and sew the crown tip lining in place. Turn in the bottom raw edge and slipstitch in place inside the crown.

❖ **PATTERN** Draw or copy your pattern at 200 per cent. Finished hat size should be approximately 7⅜in (18.5cm) at widest point of the brim by 4⅛in (10.5cm) high.

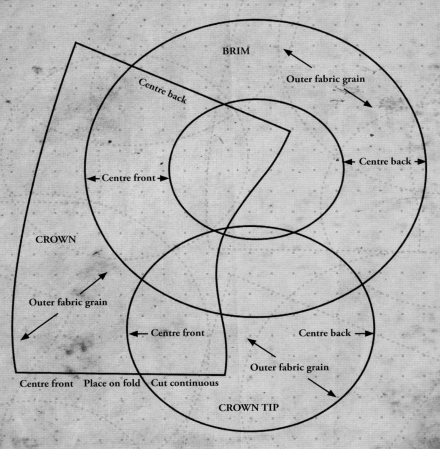

Wilhelm Lau Bregenz, Römerstr.

VAMPIRE CHATEAU

As it was getting late, I decided we should look for a nice hotel. Some greenish lights high up on a mountainside, and a suggestion of a turret against the boiling clouds, pointed the way. Streaks of eerie blue lightning flickered, showing a steep mountain path, which Mr Woppit was most reluctant to continue up. The huge door creaked open by invisible machinery as we approached and a musical voice rang out, 'Welcome, travellers.'

Standing on the stairwell was an elegant lady. Ripples of light and shadow played across her from the brazier she held in her hand, and her jewelled necklace glittered in the firelight. As she glided down the stairs, clockwork whirred and the room came to life, an army of statues emerging from the walls as an honour guard. I was immediately seized by curiosity and wished I might have an hour or two to inspect their mechanisms at my leisure.

Mr Woppit, however, was gazing entranced at the vision of loveliness before us in an attitude of complete adoration. I nudged him with my foot, remembering the unfortunate incident with the innkeeper's daughter and the wolf cub in the Carpathian Mountains.

IMMORTAL BELOVED RING

Two lovers would meet every day to play and compose beautiful music on new and strange instruments they created themselves. The birds all around the chateau would stop to listen, and mice would creep from the shadows, transfixed by the sounds of steam pipes and strings.

But the lovers were parted — quite why has been lost in the mists of time. The house was closed up and forgotten about.

Many years later, under a creaking floorboard deep inside the ancient house, a beautifully carved box was found. Inside, held in a circle of silver, was just a fragment of paper, which crumbled to dust as it opened, and yet there was a sigh in the air, a voice that whispered, 'Wherever I am, there you are also.'

IMMORTAL BELOVED RING

❖ SUPPLIES

- ¾oz (20g) slow-dry 650 silver art clay

- 2oz (50g) packet metallic polymer clay

- Tiny cogs and gears or rubber stamps with appropriate tiny motifs

- Silver polish

- Liver of sulphur patina solution

- High-temperature adhesive

❖ EQUIPMENT

- Paper ring gauges
- Ring mandrel
- Pasta machine
- Ceramic tile and water sprayer
- Tissue blade
- Spatula
- Sandpaper (240 for first sanding, 4,000 for fine sanding, 12,000 for fine polishing)
- Mould/texture plate
- Darning needle
- Scalpel or craft knife
- Wire brush

1 Measure the inside of a ring that fits using the ring-sizing papers. Wrap the guide around the mandrel, making it four sizes larger to allow for shrinkage as the clay fires. Take approximately ⅔oz (17g) of clay and roll it into a sausage shape long enough to go around the mandrel, then taper it at the ends. Wrap it around the mandrel and angle-cut at the overlap. Smooth the join completely.

2 Shape the ring roughly into the correct proportions with a spatula and leave it to dry for at least 24 hours on the mandrel somewhere warm and dry. Remove from the mandrel and, with a circular motion, sand and shape the sides flat. Keep looking at the ring's profile to make sure you get a nice even shape. Don't sand the inside of the ring or you will change the size.

3 While the ring dries, run the metallic polymer clay through the pasta machine on the thickest setting. Fold and repeat, passing the fold through first. Do this at least 20 times to align the mica particles. Place on a tile and spray with water to stop sticking. Press the tiny cogs and gearwheels or rubber stamps deep into the clay, remove and then, with the tissue blade almost flat to the clay, slice tiny slivers off to reveal the pattern.

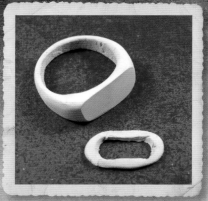

4 Place your sandpaper flat on your work surface and sand the top chunky part of the ring so it has a completely flat profile. Smooth and sand the sides and the shank to a beautiful rounded shape, leaving the top flat. The better and smoother the shape and finish before firing, the nicer the end result. Roll out a little of the leftover clay to roughly the same size as the flat top, cut a window in it and fix to the flat part as a bezel, with paste-type clay. Trim the edges flush.

5 Press a little silver clay into the mould's gear-wheel shapes, trim flush with the top and allow to dry. Re-sand the sides of the ring where the bezel is attached. Fill any holes with paste-type clay, allow to dry, then sand again. Sand the top of the bezel flat before fixing the cogs either side with paste-type clay. Allow to dry for another 12 hours. Carve the words 'Immortal beloved' on the inside of the ring with the tip of a darning needle. I used the mandrel to support the ring while working on it.

Pages from the Notebook...

This is not a difficult project, but you do need to be confident in your sculpting abilities and have plenty of patience. I always leave my chunky pieces to dry for two days, because if there is any moisture at all, the silver may crack when fired. While the piece is dry but unfired it is quite tough and sanding

is easy. It's worth investing in a good set of sanding pads or papers. I use Micro-Mesh in an assortment of grades.

Only a pasta machine will do for this project as it is aligning the mica that gives the polymer its 3D look and it needs to be rolled perfectly regularly for this to happen.

USEFUL ADVICE

When sanding the silver clay, do it over a piece of paper. Keep all the dust to make paste from, mixing a few drops of distilled water to make a thick creamy consistency that can be used as glue and filler on unfired pieces. If an unfired piece breaks while sanding, don't panic – simply glue together with paste, allow to dry thoroughly and gently sand the excess off.

Some low-fire types of silver clay can be fired with a small blowtorch rather than a kiln, so make sure you get the right clay for you.

6 Fire the silver according to the manufacturer's instructions. When completely cool, rub the white clay coating off with a wire brush, then polish to a high sheen with the superfine sandpaper and finally with silver polish. Patinate the ring with a drop of liver of sulphur in some warm water, then repolish, leaving the recesses of the cogs dark. Cut a tile of the polymer clay to the same size as the bezel, coat the underside with high-temperature glue, insert the tile and then bake according to the polymer clay manufacturer's instructions. Sand and finally polish the polymer with the superfine-grade sandpaper.

BLOOD DROP EARRINGS

'Oh goodness,' said Emilly, 'you did make me jump!'

'I think you may have dropped this, Milady.' The dashing brigand, hair cascading over his shoulders and a fringed scarf around his waist, dropped a small and intricate earring into her hand. Tiny clock hands whirred as a scarlet dewdrop formed in the centre of the filigree.

'Ouch!' she exclaimed. 'I say, do you have a pocket handkerchief I might borrow, I seem to have cut my fing...' Her voice trailed off as she looked around for the bandit, who had melted away into the darkness without a sound.

BLOOD DROP EARRINGS

❖ SUPPLIES

- 2 open Georgian drop brass blanks

- 2 open brass gearwheels

- 2 brass rivets

- 4 tiny fancy watch hands

- Resin (UV or epoxy)

- Red oil paint or resin dye

- Small reel of 0.5mm (SWG 26, AWG 25) copper-coloured wire

- 2 x 5mm dark red round crystals

- 2 x 6mm drop crystals

- 2 copper-coloured headpins

- 2 copper-coloured earring hooks

- 4 x 4mm copper-coloured jumprings

❖ EQUIPMENT

- Permanent marker pen
- Small drill or tiny hole cutter
- Round needle file
- Metal block and hammer
- Sticky tape
- Lollipop stick
- Cocktail stick
- UV light (if using UV resin)
- Round-nose pliers
- Flat-nose pliers
- Cutting pliers

1 Place an open gearwheel over one of the Georgian drops and arrange so that it just clears the open section in the centre of the panel. Mark the centre hole with a permanent marker pen, then drill the hole at the base of the brass shapes. Use a drill bit or hole cutter the same size as the rivet shaft.

2 Put the rivet's nail head at the back of the drop. Thread the gearwheel then the watch hands on. If the watch hands' holes are too small, gently file them with a round needle file. Snip the shaft of the rivet off 1/16in (2mm) above the drop. Tap gently round the edges with a hammer until the end is mushroom-shaped and holding the pieces firmly together.

3 Stick a piece of sticky tape on the back of the brass drop, rubbing and burnishing very firmly around the edge of the decorative hole to create a good seal – if there are any gaps the resin will run through. Use a tool such as the wrong end of a pencil or paintbrush to help if necessary.

Pages from the Notebook...

Setting rivets well takes time and practice but it's a skill worth acquiring. The aim is not to simply bash the head of the rivet as hard as you can, as this will just bend the head and set it at an odd angle. By tapping the sharp corners, you slowly create another domed pinhead. It only needs to be sufficiently bigger than the hole to stop the rivet pulling through. If the shaft is short you will find your piece sets tightly together. If you want something to move freely leave the shaft a little longer.

4 I used UV resin, but epoxy works just as well. Touch a cocktail stick to the top of the red oil paint and let the paint drop on to a lollipop stick. Mix a pea-sized drop of resin with the paint and drop in the brass plate hole. Allow to spread, then cure under the UV light for 15–20 minutes (or leave for 24 hours if using epoxy resin).

USEFUL ADVICE

Don't overfill the hole with resin; it's better to build up two layers of resin to get a lovely dome, letting the first cure before adding a second. Then, remove the sticky tape and do a layer on the underside too for a really lovely three-dimensional droplet.

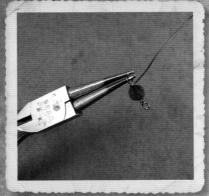

6 Join the components together. First attach the round crystal to the earring hook, twisting open and closed as you would a jumpring. Then attach the drop crystal on a headpin to the bottom of the open gearwheel, using another jumpring. Repeat the process for the other earring.

5 Using your round-nose pliers, create a wrapped loop at the end of a short piece of the wire (see page 167), then thread on one of the round crystals and make another loop at the other end. Trim all extra bits of wire neatly. Attach to the top of the drop with one of the jumprings. Thread the drop crystal onto a headpin, make another wrapped loop and trim.

QUEEN OF THE DAMNED NECKLACE

Some ancient artefacts are said to be imbued with great power — such is the necklace of Milady Szustakiewicz. Many stories are whispered about this necklace; some say that to wear it makes one immortal, though as usual, this gift comes with a terrible price. Others say the portrait ages while the gentleman it portrays does not…

Dickens and Rivett have long wanted to examine it, purely for cataloguing and completion of their records but, as yet, it has never left the family for whom it was created, merely passing from one beautiful lady to another. However, it has been noted how incredibly similar all the female descendants of this line look.

QUEEN OF THE DAMNED NECKLACE

❖ SUPPLIES

- Small vial

- Glass glitter

- Cranberry-coloured alcohol ink

- Copper-coloured headpin

- 8in (20cm) of 0.5mm (SWG 26, AWG 25) brass wire

- 1½in (4cm) smaller side filigrees

- 2 large black patinated copper cogs

- Image for the locket

- Glass cabochon to fit bezel/locket, approximately 1 x ¾in (2.6 x 1.8cm)

- Ranger's Glossy Accents or PVA glue

- Fancy bezel/locket

- Piece of filigree approximately 2in (5cm)

- About 18 x 4mm pearls, 20 x 4mm crystals, 4 x 5mm pearls and 6 x 4mm fire opal glass beads

- About 36 x 4mm brass jumprings

- About 12 x 6–8mm brass jumprings

- Decorative clasp

❖ EQUIPMENT

- Cutting pliers
- Round-nose pliers
- Flat-nose pliers

1 Fill your vial with an interesting red substance. You can make the same glitter mix as the Mortalometer (see page 126), or use thick strawberry syrup or red sparkles. Thread the headpin up through the cork and pop a dab of glue on the head part. Make a wrapped loop at the top (see page 167) and glue the cork into the bottle.

2 Use the length of brass wire to carefully secure the filigree sides to the large cog shapes. Thread the wire through any small holes in the filigree, making stitches as if you were sewing it in place with a needle and thread. Trim any excess wire flush using the cutters.

3 Print out your locket image to the correct size, or use patterned paper. Trim it carefully to the exact size of the glass cabochon. Seal it if necessary and glue to the back of the glass with Glossy Accents or PVA glue. When dry, place into the locket and close the prongs with flat-nose pliers, to hold in place.

5 Cut a 6in (15cm) length of wire. Make a wrapped loop (see page 167), then thread on a 4mm pearl, a 4mm crystal and another 4mm pearl. Make another wrapped loop on the top and trim the wire with the cutters. Create all the other components as shown in the picture, including a ¾in (2cm) length of chain by joining together alternate-sized jumprings. Join the components together with the 4mm and 5mm jumprings as shown in the image.

4 Cut another length of the wire and using the loop at the top of the cabochon locket, attach it to the central filigree petal shape. Use the round-nosed pliers to twist the wires together to secure and trim neatly. Make sure you attach the locket at the top of the diamond filigree shape.

Pages from the Notebook...

Although most printed papers work wonderfully with Glossy Accents coating, inkjet images on photo paper will bleed a bit. They can be sealed with a light coating of Renaissance wax or a quick spray of lacquer varnish, then allowed to dry for a few minutes before applying glue. I would suggest doing a test with both the glue and the paper you intend to use beforehand to check the ink won't bleed...

6 Attach each of the components to the filigree and to the cog. Note where each piece starts and ends so it will hang correctly. If you are using different filigree to mine, you may have to experiment a little to find the right places to attach.

8 Create an assortment of 10 or so wrapped loop components, making sure you have two of each kind. Link them together with 4mm jumprings and attach one end to the side filigree. Check the necklace is the right length for you and your neckline, adding more components if necessary.

7 Make up another set of the wrapped components as in step 5 and attach them together. Secure them on the other side, making sure they mirror the placing exactly of the first set. Secure the vial to the bottom of the filigree piece with a loop of three 5mm jumprings to help it hang well.

USEFUL ADVICE

If this is the first time you have tried wirework, practise your wrapped loops with scrap ends of wire to get a really good professional finish. Rather than the beaded chain, you could also attach the filigree sides to a piece of red silk ribbon, looped through in a lark's head knot and secured at the other end with a ribbon closure.

9 To finish the piece, add a decorative clasp to the other end of the glittering bead chain using jumprings of your choice. I have used a toggle clasp, but you can use any kind you like. If you have short hair it can be a lovely focal point on the back of your neck.

MORTALOMETER

The mortalometer has often been misunderstood since its invention by John Dee in 1580. Originally called a necrometer, it measures a person's life force, or vigour; not, as was often claimed by charlatans who got their hands on one, how many years were left. They are much sought after pieces of equipment for monster hunters dealing with vampires, revenants or other creatures that pass as human among us.

This glorious example is one of Bartholomew Stevenson's designs; an amateur horologist, he took to the design of gadgets and gizmos for entertainment and expeditions. Miss Ladybird often tests new pieces for him, and so was somewhat perturbed when it seemed to register very little in the way of life force in the chateau despite a whole host of gaily clad revellers dancing in the great hall.

MORTALOMETER

❖ SUPPLIES

- Large pocket watchcase

- Approximately 1 x 2in (2.5 x 5cm) shard of mica

- Very tiny gearwheels and cogs

- 2oz (50g) black polymer clay

- Brass-coloured watch chain

- Cranberry-coloured alcohol ink

- Assorted small watch parts, gearwheels, tiny screws, watch faces, cogs and crystals

- Brass-coloured toggle end

- Silver patina/painting system

- Glass glitter

- Headpins/screws

- Assorted plain and etched jumprings for fob dangles

- Large beads and charms for fob dangles

- Lobster claw clasps (optional)

❖ EQUIPMENT

- Craft knife/scalpel
- Small tub
- Cutting pliers
- Modelling tools
- Flat-ended paintbrush

1 Lay out your key pieces for the mortalometer and make a quick sketch of which objects you wish to place where. This gives you a chance to move the objects around to decide on the most pleasing composition without having to go back and undo bits after they have been stuck down.

2 Condition the black polymer clay by rolling and kneading it between your fingers until soft and pliable. Roll out enough to completely cover the inside of your case to within ¼in (5mm) of the top edge. Roughly cut it out and press inside the case using a modelling tool. Cut a deep trench with a scalpel, slightly smaller than your piece of mica (you can cut the mica with a scalpel to shape it). Peel the clay out, smooth the edges and bake at the recommended temperature for 10 minutes.

3 To dye the glass glitter, fill a small tub with the grains and drip alcohol ink onto them. Stir the grains till most are coated, then add a few more drips so the colour will vary. Leave to dry completely in a warm place. Very gently, stir the grains till they are all loose again like coloured sand.

5 Place the large main components onto the clay, adding tiny, pea-sized pieces underneath to secure them in place. If it's looking a little crowded, don't add them all. To secure the watch faces, snip the tip off a headpin, make a tiny bend at the end and thread it into the centre, pressing firmly – the hook stops it pulling out.

4 Fill the hole with a mixture of glass crystals and tiny cogs, then make a tiny strip of clay and place it all around the edge of the hole about ¹⁄₁₆in (2mm) from the edge. Lay the mica on top and press down to secure. Make another tiny strip of clay and press it to seal the edge of the mica to the strip underneath.

USEFUL ADVICE

One well-placed gearwheel is worth a dozen random scatterings… Take care how you position components; try to make them look as if they might interlock or overlap one another as you see in real machinery. Less is often more, especially if you have a particularly beautifully engraved or decorated component. Arrange them a few times and don't be afraid to use real clocks and machines for inspiration.

Pages from the Notebook…

Sculpting takes practice, and the wonderful thing is that you can always squash polymer clay flat and start again if it goes wrong. Experiment with scrap clay and tools to see what shapes and patterns you can make. Almost any household item can become a tool. Just imagine what kind of mark you want to make, then find an object that has that shape. It might be the end of a pen or pencil, a teaspoon, a broken brooch, the side of a peg, even your pliers.

6 Add more components and clay, one piece at a time, positioning them carefully. If you decide you need to leave one out because it's getting too busy or add another, that's fine. Use more tiny bits of clay to secure, sometimes going over the edges of the piece to look as if it's part of the rock. Press the modelling tool in at different angles, flattening and giving a nice texture.

8 Take up a tiny bit of silver patina or paint with the paintbrush. Wipe most of it off and gently stroke the brush over some of the raised textured areas of polymer clay to highlight. Repeat, building up layers, allowing each to dry between coats (it'll only take a few seconds) but don't overdo it. You need an almost-dry brush and subtle, shimmery layers are nicer than big blobs of silver.

7 Keep adding clay and texturing until you are completely happy with your design. Attach cogs in the same way as the watch faces, with screws or headpins. Make sure the front of the watch face still fits comfortably over your design. Press some parts down if they have got a little high. Remove the front and bake for 20 minutes at the clay manufacturer's recommended temperature.

9 To create the watch fob, attach a toggle on one end of the chain with a jumpring. Create fob dangles using charms, beads on headpins, and so on. Attach them to the chain at intervals using jumprings. If you want to be able to swap and change the fob dangles around, attach each one to a lobster claw clasp with a jumpring instead, then you can hook them on and off as you please. Attach the other end to the mortalometer.

Strunk

730 Penn St,

READING, PA.

LABYRINTH LIBRARY

Faster and faster, Mr Woppit and I raced through the forest at midnight. The moon threw odd patches of light that confused our way, and the noise of the satyr's hooves came thundering closer.

The satyr and I had got along terribly well at first, exchanging notes on stills and vintages. I had even gained some valuable tips on the brewing process and we were on our third bottle when I noticed the previously neat and ordered shelves of elegant brown leather books were looking a little ransacked.

'I told you not to read from the book!' I gasped to Mr Woppit as the sounds of our pursuit grew louder. As long fingernails or briars grabbed at my hair, which had long since escaped from its pins, I spied a doorway. It was only as it clanged shut behind us that I wondered whether that had really been the most sensible thing to do. Mr Woppit turned on his patented illuminandle and we surveyed the huge slabs of stone that lined the passageways. I could tell Mr Woppit was not going to take to my suggestion that we explored different routes, so getting out the trusty reel of thread that I always keep for repairs, and tying it to a handy nail, we set off down the gloomy maze.

RIDDLE PENDANT

So many forgotten secrets and stories are contained within the books that line the walls of the labyrinth; daring explorers who have crept the dusty paths have learned wonderful things, emerging from the shadows to set themselves up for life in the bright city, after discovering huge hoards of wealth or long-forgotten skills.

If you are ever lucky enough to find yourself within the labyrinth library, remember not to eat from any of the tempting gilded bowls, piled high with exotic fruits. Do not drink either, from any of the sweet wine-filled golden cups, lest you hear the outraged roar from the guardian of the library and are compelled to fly through the maze of bookshelves.

RIDDLE PENDANT

❖ SUPPLIES

- Photocopy of a labyrinth maze on printed-circuit-board (PCB) etching paper, overhead projector film or thin photocopier paper

- 2 x 1 ½in (5 x 4cm) sheet of copper or brass

- Alcohol wipes

- Ferric chloride etching solution and neutralizer

- Very fine opaque permanent marker pen

- Nail polish remover

- Metal patina or paint

- Approximately 4 x 4in (10 x 10cm) mica sheet

- Paper or card

- Teabag

- StazOn inkpad

- 3 jumprings and a cog

- 17–20in (42.5–50cm) chain or leather thong

❖ EQUIPMENT

- Iron
- Lolly stick
- Glass container
- Protective gloves and goggles
- Rotary tool with wire brush attachment
- Superfine-grade sandpaper or Micro-Mesh sanding pads
- Cog shapes stamp
- Paper clips
- Drill
- Hammer
- Nail
- File
- Round-nose pliers

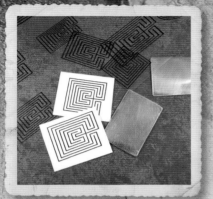

1 Photocopy or laser transfer your image onto thin photocopy paper, overhead projector film or PCB etching paper. Most office stationery suppliers will do this for you. Cut out your image to fit. Prepare your metal blank, by cleaning thoroughly and de-greasing with an alcohol wipe.

2 Dab the front of your copied image and rub the metal blank with an alcohol wipe. Place the image face down on the metal blank, cover with a piece of paper, and immediately press a hot iron onto it. Do not use steam and do not move the iron about or the image will smear. After a minute, remove the iron, cool for a moment or two and rub all over the film/paper with a lolly stick. Peel away from the metal. Redraw any missing lines or areas with the permanent marker pen.

3 Wearing protective gloves and safety goggles, prepare the etching bath according to the manufacturer's instructions and pour into a glass container (see notebook overleaf). Colour the back of the piece with an opaque permanent marker pen, so the acid doesn't etch the back, and place the metal in the bath. Etching can take between 30 minutes and 2 hours, depending on the strength and temperature of the solution and depth of line required. Remove and rinse, then dry. Clean by removing the dark toner with nail-polish remover, then polish using the wire brush attachment.

5 Cut a piece of mica and some paper or card the same size as the cover. Stain the paper with tea to make it look old and faded; make sure the edges are slightly darker, and don't forget to do both sides. On the mica and the pages, print cog shapes with the StazOn inkpad and a rubber stamp, or the solution to the maze, or a piece of poetry – whatever takes your fancy to make a personal journal.

4 Add a patina by painting on either a patinating solution, or paint over the surface, working it well into all the etched areas. Allow to develop or dry thoroughly, and then polish the colour off the raised parts with superfine sandpaper or Micro-Mesh sanding pads.

Pages from the Notebook...

BE CAREFUL! Ferric chloride is a basic acid solution that is used to etch circuit boards. You can buy it from electronic component specialists and it will etch both copper and brass. Because it is an acid, you do need to adhere to all the recommended safety procedures, so wear gloves and goggles. Also, you must not dispose of it by tipping it down the drain. You need to buy a special neutralizing powder to render it safe for disposal. There are other ways of etching, including a fascinating saltwater method, which you can find plenty of tutorials for online.

6 Layer the pages, metal blank and mica. Use paper clips to hold them together and drill three holes wide enough for your jumprings along the top edge. If you hammer a little indentation with a nail first, it will stop the drill slipping. File the holes to remove sharp edges. Thread the jumprings through the pages, with the cog at the front of one, and attach the chain or thong to hang it.

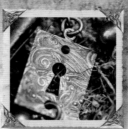

KEYS TO THE LIBRARY
KILT PIN

'Deep in the labyrinth was a huge door, 20 feet high and 10 feet across, carved and gilded with trees and strange mechanisms. Only one key could open it, and to choose the wrong one meant certain doom. Behind that door was a door, and behind that door was another door, and behind that door...'

'Oh do get on with it,' said Emilly. 'I'm bored now.'

Mr Woppit closed the huge leather-bound book in a huff and wandered off down the winding corridor. 'I wonder which door this key really does open,' mused Emilly...

KEYS TO THE LIBRARY KILT PIN

❖ SUPPLIES

- 1in (2.5cm) stampboard tile
- Dye-based inkpad
- Sponge
- Tim Holtz Distress Ink pad in Vintage Photo
- StazOn inkpad
- A small piece of filigree
- 1in (2.5cm) chain lengths
- 3.5 x 7mm nail head rivet (I used on from Vintaj)
- Metal-effect paint, such as Viva Décor Ferro
- Assorted charms (such as tiny keys, coins, keyholes, fountain pen nibs, watch parts, beads)
- Vintage key
- 2 pearl and 1 crystal bead
- About 4 x 6mm jump rings and about 5 x 4mm jumprings
- Large key blank
- 10in (25cm) x 0.5mm (SWG 26, AWG 25) copper-coloured wire
- Kilt pin

❖ EQUIPMENT

- Masking tape
- Dremel hand drill or Crop-A-Dile hole puncher
- Steampunk-themed rubber stamp
- Old pen/small scraping tool
- Drill or hole press
- Hammer
- Metal block
- Cutting pliers
- Paintbrush
- Superfine-grade sanding pad
- Metal patinas/colours
- Round-nose pliers
- Flat-nose pliers

1 Place a tiny piece of masking tape over the stamp board tile to protect the surface. Mark where you want your hole to be and make a small hole using the drill or hole puncher. Peel off the masking tape. Using a dye-based inkpad and a sponge, gently blend colour onto the tile – you can add colour in layers until you get a pleasing blend.

2 Dab a tiny bit of the Distress Ink on the corners and edges of the tile to take some of the ink colour off and make it look more vintage. Take your rubber stamp and, using the StazOn inkpad, carefully press the stamp on to the tile. Once the ink is dry, use an old pen or any small scraping tool to scratch back into the special surface of the board to give beautiful white highlights.

3 Curve a piece of filigree over the large blank key to add extra texture. Mark where the rivet will best secure the piece of filigree and make a hole with the drill or hole puncher. Hammer the filigree nice and flat around the key and thread the rivet through the key with any extra embellishments. Place the head of the rivet on a metal block, trim the stem to within $\frac{1}{16}$in (2mm) and gently set the rivet by tapping gently on the edges to make a mushroom shape, which will stop the rivet pulling back through.

4 Using a paintbrush, add metal-effect paint to any particularly shiny charms, and drill or press holes from which to hang them. Try sanding back the patinated metals to reveal the shine beneath and add texture. Found objects make wonderful personalized charms; if it's not possible to drill through them, try wrapping tightly with wire and making a wrapped loop (see page 167). Add patina and metal colours to bought pieces to make them unique too.

5 Create another wrapped loop, then thread on a bead or some crystals. Make another loop at the top and trim excess wire neatly. Attach charms to the bottom of the dangle with a jumpring. These pieces add colour and a bit of sparkle to the pin; for a more manly design, just use metal beads and spacers.

6 Hang the keys and charm lengths from the kilt pin with assorted jump rings and links of chain – arrange them all in front of you first so you can see how long they are. Try to get a variety of lengths, adding more bead components or chain as necessary.

Mr Woppit suggests...

Use your own selection of charms and found objects for a truly unique and personal piece of jewellery. Try wrapping objects with wire or filigree to provide a firm base from which to attach a jumpring or loop. Give your piece a slightly different theme, introducing different elements to your own story piece or adapting the colour scheme.

Pages from the Notebook…

Stampboard is a beautifully surfaced base for colour and pattern. It comes in a variety of sizes from tiny 'inchies' to larger pieces the size of playing cards. It is coated with clay, which absorbs the coloured inks and dyes, perfectly preserving their colour and also maintaining the crisp edges of stamps.

You can seal your finished designs with a spray lacquer (test for compatibility with inks first) and add glitter, rhinestones and other embellishments such as crackle glazes. Rather than drilling, you can glue a pendant bail to the back of stampboard, or use a piece of filigree to create a wrapped frame for it.

TWISTING IVY FASCINATOR

Once upon a time an inventor built a workshop deep in the forest. Every day he would leave the bustle of the village to sit and dream and build wonderful things, with no one but the trailing ivy for company. His sparks and solutions enveloped the cottage and made a glow that could have been seen for miles around, if anyone had looked. But one day the inventor came no more, and the creative mist soaked down into the soil around the building.

Across the inventor's long-deserted workshop the ivy crawled, grabbing little trinkets — a watch part here, a piston there. She had long ago torn down the walls, exposing the wonderful machines she had peeked in at through the window for so many years, sliding her tendrils between the stone and wood to try to reach them. When she was ready, the ivy crept inside the beautiful, shiny, metal body she had built and set off to find her beloved, a crown of leaves on her flowing green hair.

TWISTING IVY FASCINATOR

❖ SUPPLIES

- 2oz (50g) packet of green polymer clay

- 2oz (50g) packet of brown polymer clay

- 2oz (50g) packet of translucent polymer clay

- Inclusions, such as ground coffee beans, roughly crushed peppercorns, sand or grit

- Greaseproof paper

- Reel of 0.4mm (SWG 28, AWG 27) silver wire

- 6–10 tiny clock parts

- Silver tiara band

- About 18 cream freshwater pearl beads, about 20 mother of pearl tumble chip beads and about 30 jade tumble chip beads

- Packet of 0.6mm (SWG 24, AWG 23) green paper-covered flower wires

❖ EQUIPMENT

- Coarse cheese grater
- Pasta machine or acrylic rolling pin
- Embossing ivy leaf sugar-craft cutters in two sizes
- Cutting pliers
- Round-nose pliers
- Soft cloth or buffing wheel
- Permanent marker pen and a pencil

1 Mix up five or six different shades and translucencies of polymer clay. You will want a large walnut-sized lump of each mix. Add a pinch of a different inclusion to three of the mixtures. Form them into sausage shapes and press together to make a solid chunk with the tip of each colour showing.

2 Coarsely grate the whole block and gently press the flakes together to make a sheet about ¼in (5mm) thick. Roll it through the pasta machine to even it up. Start with a very wide setting, fold the clay in half and roll it through at right angles to its original direction, fold again and roll, turning as before. If using a rolling pin, follow the same process of folding in half and turning.

3 Roll until it is ¹⁄₁₆–⅛in (2–3mm) thick. Lay the sheet on a piece of greaseproof paper. Cut out two sizes of ivy, embossing each piece as you go. My tiara has nine large leaves and four small ones. Cut the paper-covered wire into enough 3in (7.5cm) lengths to match the number of leaves. Make a little hook shape on the end of each and gently push it in the centre of each ivy leaf as a stalk, then smooth the clay back over the hole. Twist or bend each leaf a little to make it look realistic. Bake according to the manufacturer's instructions. When the leaves are cool, rub them to a shine with a soft cloth or buffing wheel.

4 Cut a length of wire approx. 8in (20cm) long and thread a pearl bead to the middle. Fold the wire over the pearl and, holding the two wires close to the bead in your left hand, gently twist the pearl with your right. Don't over-twist or the wire will snap. Keep twisting until you have about 1in (2.5cm) of twisted wire, separate each strand then repeat the process to form three branches each with a pearl.

5 Make the other components by threading on a pearl to another 8in (20cm) length of wire, bend the wire around the bead then pass both wire ends through a mother of pearl tumble chip bead, adding a jade bead onto one wire and twisting again. Using more 8in (20cm) wire lengths, thread on four or five pieces of jade or jade and pearls mixed, loop into a circle then twist the wires together.

6 Make some twirly ivy creepers by creating a little hook shape at the end of a green wire with your round-nosed pliers, and then wrap the wire tightly in a spiral around a pencil. Gently remove and ease it into a loose spring shape. Twirl the wires of the other components too to give everything a springy growing look.

Mr Woppit suggests...

When attaching components to the band, it is much easier to add wire as you go along rather than trying to work with a huge long piece at the start. Wire is very forgiving and will happily stay in place with just a few tight turns. Do make sure you trim any loose ends properly though – you don't want them to scratch or get caught.

7 Lay all your leaves, spirals and other components out in front of you; make sure you have a central point and a similar number of things on each side. Find the centre point of the tiara band and mark it with a permanent marker pen. Cut a length of wire 15in (37.5cm) long and wrap several times around the centre point to secure.

9 When all the components are in place, anchor a piece of wire to one side of the band where the components finish, thread on some tumble chips, beads, clock parts and so on and wrap it between the components, pushing the beads to the front, to cover the tiara band. Wrap the remaining plain wire around the band tightly and trim neatly to finish. Twist and arrange all the components into a pleasing shape.

8 Make a 90-degree bend in each component's wire (except the springs), leaving each piece about 2–2½in (5–6cm) long, then trim the bottom section of wire to 2in (5cm). Start in the centre and bind the components tightly to the band with the long wire length, leaving only millimetres between the addition of another component, and overlapping the wires at the back of the tiara band. Place some components above the band and some below.

USEFUL ADVICE

Use the jade-tumble chips to give you a starting point for your
polymer clay colours. Make them all fairly different but complementary
tones – in pieces of real jade you can really see the different strata.
The more realistic your faux ivy-leaf colours are compared to the
original stone-tumble chips, the better the piece will look. Add
the brown 'inclusions' very sparingly to change the primary colour
of the greens and mix well before adding more.

LEATHER PUZZLE BRACER

There is a place in the wood where the trees grow close together. Little light reaches the giant feet of the trees, though unwary travellers may find ferns beginning to twirl up an ankle if they stand still too long.

If you are brave enough to venture into this dark place, you may hear echoing laughter and the sound of hooves just out of view. If you are unlucky you may feel an arrow whiz past your ear. Then you must run as fast and as far as you can, for to be elf shot is a terrible thing indeed.

Lord Malmsey's aunt loves to corner people at parties and bore them about how she was elf shot in her youth. After half an hour of lurid, detailed descriptions of the symptoms, most people feel they'd rather have taken the arrow themselves.

LEATHER PUZZLE BRACER

❖ SUPPLIES

- Approximately 18in (46cm) square of thick brown leather or synthetic alternative

- 16 x 2-part leather rivets (4 with slightly longer shanks)

- 4 buckles for ¾in (2cm) straps

- 8 decorative split pins

- Brass keyhole plate

- Additional decoration as desired

◆ EQUIPMENT

- Pattern paper or a photocopier
- Craft knife or very sharp scalpel
- ⅛in (3mm) leather hole punch
- Hammer
- Sandbag or wooden curved former
- Drill (if plate has no holes)

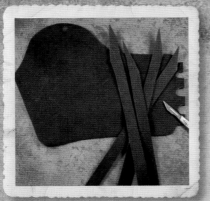

1 Photocopy the pattern on page 163 at 200 per cent or scale it up to double the size using pattern paper. Cut out the pattern and use it to cut out the main large leather bracer piece with the scalpel or craft knife. Also cut out four strips of leather ¾in (2cm) by 6in (15cm). Work slowly and carefully; leather can be awkward to cut. Mark on all the placements for buckles.

2 Shape the ends of the straps to V-shaped points. Place each strap on the bracer piece as shown in the photo, overlapping by about 1in (2.5cm). Hold firmly in place while you punch a hole right through both layers and set a two-part rivet. Punch another hole next to the first one and set another rivet through it. Do this for all four straps.

3 Cut out four strips of leather ¾in (2cm) by 6½in (2.5cm) for the buckle pieces and cut the ends to points. Shape the centre sections as shown to suit your buckles, then punch three holes, one right in the middle and one in the centre of each pointed end. Thread on the buckle, inserting the prong through the middle hole.

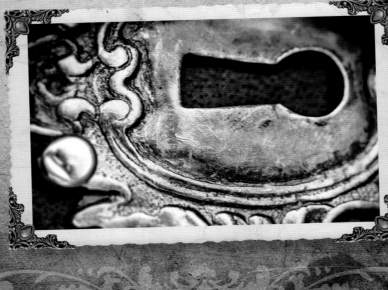

5 Punch holes halfway along the straps and insert the split pins for decoration, two on each strap. You could also use a decorative rivet for a different look. Punch holes at the ends of the straps to allow the buckles to be done up.

4 Try the bracer on and check the positioning of the buckles. Punch holes where marked on the pattern for the buckles. Fold the leather of the buckle strap in half and rivet in place with the two-part rivets again, using the rivets with a slightly longer shank to get through all three leather layers.

Mr Rivett suggests...

Laser-cutting services are perfect for adding intricate patterns into leather. Check on the internet or in the telephone book for services near you. Once the pattern is designed in an art program such as Illustrator, the laser cutter can burn it into the leather. It can cut out the pattern completely leaving a lace-like texture, or it can simply engrave the pattern into it, leaving a design more like pyrography. Because leather doesn't fray, very delicate, precise decoration can be made.

6 Curve the keyhole plate by hammering on the side edges inside while the front is supported by a sandbag or wooden curved former; it doesn't need much of a curve – just enough to follow the bracer round the arm. Position and mark holes for the rivets if there aren't some already drilled, then drill these through the plate. Punch the leather. Set the rivets, adding more decorative pieces as desired.

USEFUL ADVICE

There are many types of leather. I have used a pre-dyed thick but fairly supple type, and you could also use unprepared leather such as vege-tan and dye it yourself with leather dyes. This gives you the option to shade colours, even airbrush shades of dye across the leather, or through stencils. It is also possible to add shine and slight variations in colour by polishing pre-dyed leather with shoe polish! Leather is very easy to work with – just make sure you try out patterns in card first to avoid expensive mistakes.

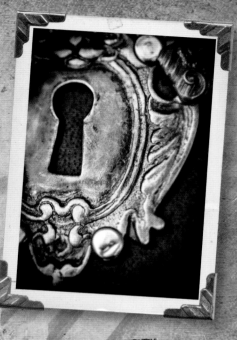

❖ PATTERN
Scale pattern up to 200 per cent. Actual shape should be 11⅜in (29cm) by 9½in (24cm) at the widest points.

Placement for buckles

EMBARK ON YOUR STEAMPUNK ADVENTURE

In Emilly's workshop, tools and gemstones jostle for position with diagrams and pictures of rocket ships and curious beasts. There is glue galore and pencil sketches and designs for amazing artefacts on the back of old envelopes, and jam jars full of cogs, screws and bits of wire. For Emilly never throws anything away – she keeps it carefully in a safe place for, after all, you never know when it may come in useful!

Are you feeling inspired? In this section of the library you will find the basic techniques and ideas you will need for creating truly unique and individual pieces. There are also useful places to find materials and equipment.

Always practise the basic techniques thoroughly, and familiarise yourself with any tools or supplies you've not used before to gain the most professional results for your creations, then you'll be ready for creative exploration too!

BASIC TECHNIQUES

HEAD PIN LOOP

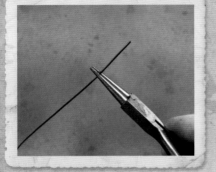

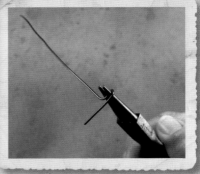

1 Using round-nose pliers, grip your piece of wire about 1in (2.5cm) from the top.

2 Twist the pliers through 90 degrees away from you, creating a right angle in the wire.

3 With your free hand, curve the top piece of wire back towards you, shaping it tightly over the top of the pliers.

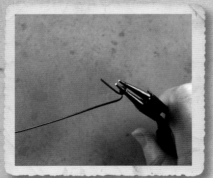

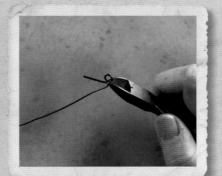

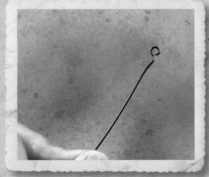

4 Keep curving the wire until it crosses the other piece of wire. Remove the round-nose pliers from the wire loop.

5 Slide the cutting pliers inside the loop so the cutting edge is flush with the inside edge of the wire circle, and snip.

6 And that's it – your headpin loop is now ready to use.

WRAPPED LOOP

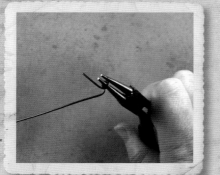

1 Follow steps 1–4 of making a headpin loop (left).

2 Grip the loop you have made with flat-nose pliers.

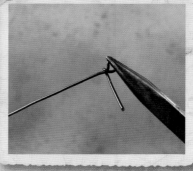

3 Start wrapping the tail around the stem wire very neatly.

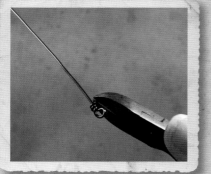

4 Wrap three times close together, then snip close to the stem.

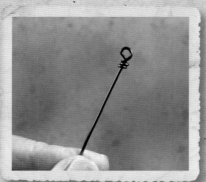

5 Your wrapped loop is now ready to use in your steampunk creations.

OPENING AND CLOSING A JUMPRING

Hold each side of the ring with a pair of pliers and twist one forward and one backwards. Do not pull the ends apart because it will not return to a perfect circle. To close, grip each side with pliers and twist back again.

PATINAS AND PAINT

There are loads of different ways to colour polymer clay, and many of these can also be used with metal filigree or embossed metal shapes for wonderful effects. Patina solutions react with metal or a metal coating, causing a chemical reaction that changes the colour and often the texture too. Verdigris on copper is an example of this.

These baked polymer clay rabbits (see opposite) have each been painted with a different metal base coat, then a patina solution was applied in some areas and finally a wash of transparent dye from the Swellegant! range.

There are plenty of possible interesting combinations, each with its own effect and colouring. The results are often a little unpredictable, so it's important to have a relaxed attitude to the effects and do trial pieces before committing to your final item.

Other colouring on metal can be achieved by paints designed specifically for metal, such as the Vintaj patinas or enamel paints. You can even use nail varnish. Baked polymer clay can be painted afterwards with acrylic paints and re-baked just for five minutes or so to 'set' the paint.

Alcohol inks can be used to provide a lovely layer of transparent dye colour on practically any surface, almost like a wash of watercolour.

All these surface treatments need to be sealed if they aren't to deteriorate over time. Swellegant! has its own sealant, but for the others you can use a silicone wax such as Renaissance wax or you can apply a varnish that is compatible with both your base material and the paint. Always do a small test piece; sometimes the manufacturers change the ingredients and something that was compatible before no longer is.

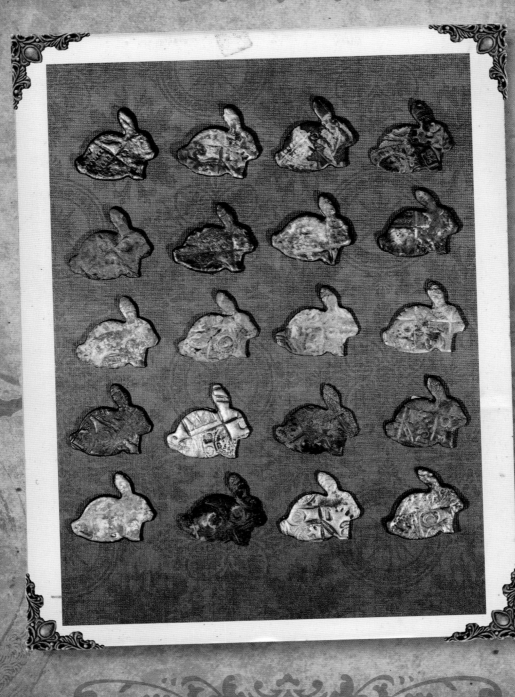

A very wide range of results can be achieved using different base coats, patina solutions and dyes.

UNLEASH YOUR CREATIVITY

There are just so many ways to use all the techniques you have learned in this book. Each project can be altered just a little by adding your own beads, charms or images to really put your own unique stamp on each piece.

Many people interested in steampunk have an alternate persona that they use on forums and message boards, and at conventions. Sometimes these characters have a whole back story to them; sometimes they are just a whimsical name. Either way, you can reflect this persona in the accessories you make.

Creating a name and a persona is a wonderful start to embarking on your steampunk adventure. This is fantasy, remember, so you can adopt a Victorian profession entirely different from your own and as extraordinary as you like. You could be a moon opal importer, an engineer aboard an intergalactic luxury liner, a gentleman inventor or a lady writer! Just think about the steampunk universe and your place within it. Then think about

the thing you want to make as an extension of the character. What are the subtle extra clues to identity you'd like to play with? Perhaps wing motifs or zeppelins for an airship pilot, scarabs for an Egyptologist, delicate pieces for a debutante, and solid workmanlike pieces for a craftsman – there are so many themes to choose from.

CHOOSING COLOURS

Think about your colour palette.
You might want to create a piece
to accessorize an outfit you already
own, or try a colour combination
you haven't used before. I often use
a colour wheel or random pages torn
from flower catalogues to inspire new
combinations. Nature rarely creates
unpleasant mixes of colour – though
there are sometimes surprising ones.

Plan your colours and your character
motifs before you start. Maybe even do
a little test piece first, and then relax,
have fun and enjoy the imperfections
and quirks that will make your piece
unique. Don't forget to look out for
surprising new ways of doing things
and happy accidents too!

A basic colour wheel has the three
primary colours of yellow, blue and
red. Secondary colours are made from
mixing each of them and tertiary
colours from mixing those.

Analogous colours are any three colours
that are side by side, such as green,
green-blue and blue. These analogous
colours make a soft and gentle, safe and
pleasing combination, like those in the
Mermaid Earrings.

Complementary colours are any two
colours that are directly opposite
each other, such as green and red, or
blue-purple and yellow-orange. These
complementary colours zing in an
eye-catching way when placed next to
each other; the Mini Top Hat is a good
example of this.

A tertiary colour wheel

RESOURCES

Here's where you can find the products used throughout the book. Most of these companies will ship supplies internationally. If you have problems locating anything, just come and ask me for suggestions at **www.facebook.com/emillyladybird**

Angelina fusible film
www.craftynotions.com
www.fredaldous.co.uk

Beading wire
www.beadsdirect.co.uk
www.beadwork-supplies.com
www.softflexcompany.com

Dip It Fantasy Film
www.fredaldous.co.uk

Etching supplies
www.maplin.co.uk
www.jameco.com

Filigree, charms and metal findings
www.bsueboutiques.com
www.rings-things.com
www.vintaj.com
cforiginals.net

Geomfix clay
www.geomfix.com

Glossy Accents clear gloss medium
www.rangerink.com

Golden Gel Medium
www.goldenpaints.com
www.pegasusart.co.uk

Ink pads, stamps and inks
www.cardcraft-uk.co.uk
www.rangerink.com
www.tsukineko.com
shop.paperartsy.co.uk

Jones Tones Foil Paper
www.jonestones.com

Leather supplies
www.leprevo.co.uk
www.tandyleatherfactory.com

Metallic-effect paint
www.viva-decor.us/ferro

Patina solutions
cforiginals.net
www.hodgepodgerie.com

Perfect Pearls Pigment Powder
www.rangerink.com

Plain metal cuffs and shapes
www.beadwork-supplies.com

Polymer clay and accessories
www.polymerclay.co.uk

Renaissance wax
www.goldleafsupplies.co.uk

Shrink plastic and printable films
www.grafixarts.com

Silver clay, epoxy clay and tools
www.metalclay.co.uk

StazOn inkpads
www.tsukineko.com

Swellegant! patinas
cforiginals.net

Tim Holtz Distress Ink pad
www.rangerink.com

Vials, bezels, acrylic domes, beetle wings and other odds and ends
www.etsy.com
www.ebay.co.uk

Vintaj products
www.vintaj.com

GLOSSARY

Absinthe A bright green, high-alcohol spirit, flavoured with aniseed, fennel, wormwood and other botanicals, popular in the mid-1800s.

Acrylic brayer A small non-stick plastic rolling pin.

Bezel A solid-backed frame, which can be filled with a picture or flooded with resin.

Buckram A glue-stiffened hessian fabric, similar in weight and thickness to card.

Cutting pliers Used for snipping wire (never use scissors instead of pliers – you will blunt them).

Eyepin A length of wire with a round eye, pre-shaped at one end, useful for adding beads and attaching together for a decorative chain.

Flat-nose pliers The best choice for holding and gripping flat things and making right angles in wire.

Filigree An intricate copper or brass metal shape with lots of open, lace-like decorative spaces.

Headpin A piece of wire that is pre-shaped with a flat head at one end, like a blunt flexible pin, used for threading beads on for earring and necklace dangles.

Jumpring A wire ring of various sizes and metals, cut flush in one place on the circle, so it can be twisted open and closed to join components.

Kraken A fearsome and mythical beast of the sea, possibly a cross between a whale and a giant squid.

Liver of sulphur patina solution A chemical used to tarnish silver.

Lobster clasps Simple oval clasps that open and close with a spring.

Loop and toggle clasp A decorative toggle through a ring, often made from intricate metalwork or beaded.

Mica A naturally occurring transparent substance, found either as a sheet, or as a powder, dyed to give an iridescent sheen.

Oberon, King of the Fae A powerful and magical lord, alluded to by Shakespeare and Merovingian legend.

Patina solution see liver of sulphur patina solution.

Round-nosed pliers For creating loops and rounded shapes in wire.

Satyr A creature from Greek mythology; half man, half goat. Fond of wine and wild parties.

Shot silk If the warp and weft threads of a piece of silk are two or more colours, the fabric subtly changes shade when viewed at different angles and in different lights.

GATHERINGS AND INFORMATION

Miss Emilly Ladybird's Facebook page
www.facebook.com/emillyladybird

The Victorian Steampunk Society (UK)
www.thevss.yolasite.com

Brass Goggles Steampunk Forum (international)
www.brassgoggles.co.uk/forum

Online magazine 'The Steampunk Chronicle'
www.steampunkchronicle.com

One of the many Steampunk facebook groups, have a look for some in your area too!
www.facebook.com/SteampunkSteampunk

ACKNOWLEDGEMENTS

Gold stars are to be awarded to my photographer Martin SoulStealer and my digital artist Terry Lightfoot.

The silver cup is presented to the wonderful models: Matt Broom, Enys Coggles, Kit Cox, Nik Hewitt, Heather Macdonald, Claire Peacey, Frances Rockett, Lyssa Ryan, Kate Vigurs-Broom and Ruth Watkin.

Certificates of merit all round for the team at GMC Publications.

Best in Show goes to friends, assistants, inspirers and enthusers: Kim Mack, Joanna Barchett, Sue Corrie, Lynne Hardy and Emma Brackenbury.

For Denise Piggin and Lee Edward Armstrong a rousing hurrah for the creation of the fairy horns and headdresses, and the loan of his neck respectively.

And tea and cake all round to the lovely fans that make being Emilly Ladybird such fun!

INDEX

To order a book, or to request
a catalogue, contact:

GMC Publications Ltd
Castle Place, 166 High Street,
Lewes, East Sussex,
BN7 1XU
United Kingdom
Tel: +44 (0)1273 488005
www.gmcbooks.com